Ellie Rohm

A DIET OF POISON

Surviving a childhood of cruelty

Ellie Rohm
A DIET OF POISON
Surviving a childhood of cruelty

MEREO
Cirencester

Mereo Books

1A The Wool Market Dyer Street Cirencester Gloucestershire GL7 2PR
An imprint of Memoirs Publishing www.mereobooks.com

A DIET OF POISON: 978-1-86151-554-4

First published in Great Britain in 2015
by Mereo Books, an imprint of Memoirs Publishing

Copyright ©2015

Ellie Rohm has asserted her right under the Copyright Designs and Patents Act 1988 to be identified as the author of this work.

A CIP catalogue record for this book is available from the British Library.

This book is sold subject to the condition that it shall not by way of trade or otherwise be lent, resold, hired out or otherwise circulated without the publisher's prior consent in any form of binding or cover, other than that in which it is published and without a similar condition, including this condition being imposed on the subsequent purchaser.

The address for Memoirs Publishing Group Limited can be found at
www.memoirspublishing.com

The Memoirs Publishing Group Ltd Reg. No. 7834348

The Memoirs Publishing Group supports both The Forest Stewardship Council® (FSC®) and the PEFC® leading international forest-certification organisations. Our books carrying both the FSC label and the PEFC® and are printed on FSC®-certified paper. FSC® is the only forest-certification scheme supported by the leading environmental organisations including Greenpeace. Our paper procurement policy can be found at www.memoirspublishing.com/environment

Typeset in 10/15pt Century Schoolbook
by Wiltshire Associates Publisher Services Ltd. Printed and bound in Great Britain by Printondemand-Worldwide, Peterborough PE2 6XD

Chapter One

I was at my happiest playing by myself, talking to my imaginary friends. I could spend hours on my own and then a voice would call, 'Ellie, where are you?' A shiver would run through me. Mother was summoning me to do my chores.

If I didn't do it right, I got a kick or slap around my face. 'You stupid girl! Can't you do it right?' Slap! My ears would burn for a long time.

I was unfortunate enough to be born a girl, and out of wedlock. At that time, girls were not welcome in my native country of Austria, especially as the firstborn.

The room we lived in was on the first floor of a very old house. The wooden stairs were dangerously worn. It was a dingy place, and there wasn't much space. All we had was a bed, a chest of drawers, a two-seater bench, a chair and a wood-burning stove. I slept in a little cot in the corner. There was no electric light in those days.

At the back of the house was a yard, and in one corner stood the kennel where our St Bernard bitch lived with her puppies. If I wanted to get away from my mother I would crawl in with the dog and her puppies. I was safe there: the dog wouldn't let anyone near her pups or me, so no one could get to me. Mother was always bad-tempered; it felt as though all the frustration she felt in her life was directed towards me.

Mother's day would start at five in the morning. She would make breakfast and get my dad up for work, on the days he was home. At six o'clock he caught his bus to Klagenfurt where he worked.

I don't remember much about my father. He worked away all week and only came home at weekends. He was a bricklayer by trade, and a good one at that. Every Friday evening he would walk two miles from the bus stop to get to our village.

As soon as he got home he and Mother would argue, mainly over money – or the lack of it. Mother would never see a penny of his earnings. To feed herself and me she had to work for the farmer from whom we rented the room. She would lock me in the room or take me with her into the fields where she worked. Most of the time I was locked in.

Father would spend all weekends in the gasthaus, drinking schnapps and playing cards with his mates. By Sunday lunchtime he was so drunk he could barely stagger home. Most of the time he would have lost all his hard-earned money gambling. Mother could barely hold her temper, and as soon as Father walked through the door she would spit in his face. Father was in no mood for a fight – all he wanted was to eat his lunch and then go to bed and sleep it off. But Mother wasn't going to let that happen. Dishes went flying, and I would hide under the table. I remember on one occasion Father picked up the chair – our only chair – and aimed it at mother's head. It just missed her head but instead struck her shoulder and back. But still she shouted abuse at him. She just could not leave it alone. Father threw the chair onto the floor and walked out of the house. I crawled out from under the table and hugged her.

I was three years old when, one Saturday morning, my mother called me. 'Ellie,' she said, 'go to the gasthaus in Sittich and bring your father home. Run! Be quick, and don't hang about.' I could see she was in terrible pain, but I had no idea what was causing it.

It was a sunny November morning, but there was a frost on the ground. I went out in a thin coat and slippers to fetch my father.

There was only one gasthaus in that village, about a mile or so away. I ran all the way, as fast as my little legs could carry me. When I got there, I looked through the glass door into the kitchen. And there was father with his friends. They were sitting around a large kitchen table, quite drunk. He had been there since Friday night. He had his playing cards in his left hand and a drink in his right.

To get to him I had to pass a huge stone oven. On top of that oven was a platform, and on that platform lay a man who had passed out, his face as red as a beetroot. I thought he was dead. I was so frightened I could not move. It was a long time before I could get that face out of my mind.

'What are you doing here?' my father shouted.

'M-mama sent me, Dada.' I stuttered. 'Please come home quick. Mama is on the floor crying.' I was pulling his jacket sleeves.

He had no intention of coming away from his game, but I persisted.

Father and I staggered home – or, rather, he was doing the staggering. He was in a loathsome mood, having been dragged away from his game, which would normally have gone on until Sunday lunchtime. He was very drunk and very angry by the time we got home.

'What the devil took you so long?' Mother shouted between labour pains. 'Couldn't you drag yourself away from your harlots?' Father was well known for his womanising. It was an accusation that came up with every argument they had. And every time it was like a red rag in front of a raging bull.

'I don't think for one moment that brat you're carrying is mine,' my father shouted, and he gave her a mighty kick, right in her swollen stomach. He was still wearing his hobnail boots that he wore for work every day.

I was so frightened I ran out the door and down the creaking stairs. I could hear my mother screaming with pain for hours. I eventually went to sleep with the puppies.

Chapter Two

In the morning when I awoke, I crawled out of the kennel and went looking for my parents. But the house was empty. Our next-door neighbour took me in. I was told my mama had gone to the hospital as she was badly hurt.

I was happy with the next door neighbour. I played with their boys, who were of a similar age to me. I cried when my father eventually came home.

'Ellie,' my father said, 'we are going on a long journey to see your grandmother.'

I said, 'But I want to see Mama,' and cried again. Of course, it was no use protesting: I had to do what I was told. Father bundled my few bits and pieces together and we set off for my grandmother's (my mother's mother).

There was no bus or train that would take us to my grandmother's house, and there was a very large mountain to climb along the way. It took three and a half hours. I was only three years old, and the going was very slow. Father had to carry me and my belongings for much of the way.

The mountain we had to climb was called Goldin. A hundred years earlier it had been mined for gold. The mine shafts were still visible. It was creepy. There were tunnels, where rusty water would seep from the rock walls. We had to spend a night in those tunnels. We couldn't travel through the night – it would be easy to get lost in the forest.

My grandparents' smallholding was another half day away, after we had climbed the mountain, but the land had evened out and the going was easier.

When we arrived, Grandmother was none too friendly. She did not like girls, and neither did she like my father. But there was no alternative: I had to stay with her. No one else would have me.

Father was eager to get away. He had a long journey back. But I clung to his long legs. 'Please don't leave me here!' I cried. I had been torn from my home, albeit a violent one. But it was the only home I knew.

Grandmother's kitchen alone was bigger than the one room that was our home. The large stove where Grandmother did all the cooking also kept the room warm. On the wall was a clock with a long pendulum that swung to and fro, and in the corner was a wall shelf with a birdcage on it. Grandfather kept two white doves in that cage.

I met my Aunty Angie for the first time. She was my mother's half-sister. I also met my half-brother, who was three years older than I was.

I loved my Aunty Angie. I remember she would carry me to bed every night. She made my stay there much more bearable.

But as for my half-brother Val, he was a naughty, spiteful and devious boy, and he was very cruel to me. On one occasion, when he was doing his homework, he said, 'Open your hand out flat – I'll show you a trick.' He picked up his pencil and pushed the sharp end through my palm.

Once a month my father came to visit for the weekend. I would walk half a mile down the road to meet him. We would spend Saturday and Sunday together. I was so happy to see him.

When the time came for him to leave, I would beg him to take me with him. I desperately wanted to go with him away from this place, away from these people who did not love me.

Grandfather worked on the railway so the farm was mainly run by Gran and Aunty Angie. Val and I also had chores to do, feeding the chickens and herding the cows.

At the bottom of the field was a river, and beyond that was woodland where Grandfather would fell timber for winter fuel. There was an old woman who would help with the logging. One day she was hit by one of the heavy branches. She died there in the woods. There was nothing anyone could do – she had just got in the way.

Val and I got into much mischief. By the river was an old wooden hut where an old man lived with his dog, Lydie. We tormented that old man to distraction. We would throw stones on his roof and then run away. He would come running out of his hut, waving a stick and would set the dog on us. It was all right for Val, he had longer legs than I did. I barely got away.

My mother, Maria Draghashnig, was illegitimate. Her father was rumoured to be a jailbird drifter who seduced my grandmother. Mother was an unwanted child, and her mother hated her with a vengeance. But Angie, who was ten years younger than my mother, was loved and very spoiled.

When Grandfather married Gran, he adopted my mother, so mother and Aunty Angie were half-sisters, but they did not get on. There was much jealousy between them. Grandfather was always good to my mother, but that did not sit well with Aunty Angie or Gran.

When Mama was eighteen years old she became involved with an older man and had two children with him. The first was a girl, but sadly she died when she was a year old. Then she had Val, in 1929. Mother was very happy with this man. But he caught tuberculosis and died soon after Val was born.

Mother was strapped for money. She had to find work – any work. She had no choice but to leave Val with Grandmother, who brought him up. That is why Val was so jealous of me, as I had a mother and he had none. Val had been told that his mother didn't want him, but that was not true. It was my father who did not want Val living with us.

Mother met my father, Friedrich, in the town of Klagenfurt. He was instantly attracted to her, and she to him. Friedrich was a very handsome man: he had dark hair, sexy brown eyes, an olive complexion and a toothbrush moustache.

From the moment they met they had a love–hate relationship. Every time Maria tried to get away from him, he was one step behind her.

Friedrich would give her money – for herself and to pay her mother for looking after Val. She always intended to repay him, but she never could. Every time she broke away from him he demanded his money back.

She went to work in another town, far away from him. She was gone for more than a year, but had to come back to see Val and to give her mother some money for looking after him.

While working away she had bought herself some good quality, expensive clothes, including a winter coat. It was navy blue with a beautiful fur collar. But when she got home, her half-sister Angie stole the coat from her. It did nothing to improve their relationship.

Now that she was back in Klagenfurt and looking for work, it was inevitable that Maria would bump into Friedrich at some time. It was as if her future was mapped out for her: she just couldn't get away from him.

The love–hate relationship they had never changed. Maria would be jealous when Friedrich even looked at another woman, and he if she so much as looked at another man. That was the start of every argument they ever had - that and money, of course.

Maria discovered very early in their relationship that Friedrich was cruel, mean, hard-drinking and quick-tempered – and there was no getting away from him.

But he was so very handsome, with his dreamy brown eyes and black curly hair. Women couldn't help but fall in love with him.

In February 1932 my mother fell pregnant with me. Her fate was sealed: they had to set up home together. I was born on 5th November 1932.

The village I was born in was called Maltchach. It consisted of a handful of houses and the large farmhouse where my mother worked every day, as well as the one-roomed cottage where I remember having been locked in for most of the day while my mother was at work.

Chapter Three

After leaving my grandmother's house, Father told me, 'Ellie, when we get home your Mama will be there waiting for us. And you also have a little brother. His name is Englbert.'

Mama had been away for a whole year, and when we finally got home, I found her walking on crutches, as she would be for some time to come. After my father had kicked her while she was in labour, she had developed tetanus poisoning all over her body. She continued to need the crutches for a year after she came home from the hospital, so we had to move to a cottage that had no stairs.

Baby Englbert was now one year old. He was a fat little thing with white-blonde hair.

We went home to the same village, but to a different cottage. Our new home was right at the end of the village, all on its own, with no neighbours.

'Friedrich, isn't it about time you gave me some housekeeping money?' Mother said.

'You shut your mouth, woman.' And with it came a slap. She was too weak still to defend herself.

I knew it wouldn't end there. I hid under the bed. Englbert was crying in his cot. Mother just wouldn't leave it alone – she would aggravate Father's temper to such a pitch, until she was on the floor in a pool of blood.

I hated my father for this violence.

On warm summer mornings I would go outside the cottage. On one occasion I came across a large snake. Mother said it was an adder. She gathered me into her arms and put me down at a safe distance.

'Are you going to kill it, Mama?' I asked.

'Oh no,' she said. 'They eat all the rats and mice around the cottage,' so she let it gently slide away.

All around our cottage were fields and meadows, as far as the eye could see. At the bottom of our meadow was a large lake, Lake Maltchach.

Mr Unterweger was the cabinet maker. His house, workshop and villa stood very close to the schoolhouse at the bottom of our hill. One winter Mother asked him to make us a sledge, which he did. It was nothing much to look at and very lightweight, but it travelled very fast.

We would sledge down the meadow. One day I hit a tree, head on at full speed. All my front teeth were knocked out, and I had a dent in my head and a broken arm.

Nothing changed. The arguments and fights never stopped. Every weekend, as regular as clockwork, Father came home from work, had a wash and shave, put on his Sunday best and couldn't get to the gasthaus quick enough.

No money was ever put on the table for food or clothing. After a year, when Mother was able to walk without the crutches, she went back to work for the farmer to earn money to feed us. My brother and I wore dresses that had been cut down from Mother's old dresses.

One day in spring 1938, Mother packed our few belongings into a rucksack. We set off early in the morning to catch a train. It was a seven-kilometre walk into the town. I was five years old and Englbert was two. We were running away from Father. When he came home on Friday night he would find the cottage empty.

When we got off the train, I didn't recognise any of the landscape. Mother did not give us any details about where we were going. We simply got off the train and started walking.

We walked until we came to a crossroads. The left turning would take us into the mountains, but Mother didn't know that, and that was the road we took. We started walking away from the direction we should have taken.

I was used to walking; we do a lot of walking in the country, from village to village, as they are often quite far apart. But my little brother Englbert had to be carried, and was quite heavy.

My mother had a strong will, and she was determined to get as far away as possible from the quarrels and beatings, from the breaking of furniture every week.

We walked and walked and walked. The road was deserted. There was not a soul to be seen – no cars, no horses or carts; no one but Mother, Englbert and me.

Mother was so sure she had taken the right turn at the crossing. The sun was bright and hot, and Englbert was whimpering from sheer exhaustion and hunger. I watched as Mother's mood changed to one of despair. I knew from experience that this was a dangerous time to be around her.

Eventually she realised that we had taken the wrong turning at the crossroads many miles back. She fell to her knees and cried, 'Dear God, send us help.' We were all so tired and just couldn't go any further.

We stood by an iron railing, and I could hear a raging river nearby. Mother stood up very slowly. I knew what she was going to do.

She picked me up and held me over the iron railing. She was about to throw me over into that fast-moving, green, cold river.

'Please, Mama, don't throw me into that cold water,' I begged. 'Please don't kill me.'

Coming to her senses and realising what she had been just about to do, she pulled me back and put me back down on the road.

We were all trembling, crying together and hugging one another.

'Holy Mother of God, please help us in this hour of need.' Mother was on her knees, praying, with tears running down her face. We were a desperate bunch, huddled together in the middle of the dirt road to nowhere.

There was only one way to go, and that was back, all the way back to the crossing, back the way we had come.

All we could hear was the deafening sound of the river as it flowed beneath us. But suddenly we began to hear another sound – the sound of a motor car. Not many people had cars in those days: you could wait all day before seeing even one car. Yet to our disbelief and sheer delight, it was coming our way.

Mother stood up and, with frenzied arms flapping, she shouted, 'Please stop!'

The man stopped his car. 'Where are you going on this deserted stretch of road?' he asked.

'I need to get to Spittal an der Drau with my children. I have a post there as a housekeeper,' Mother replied.

'Dear lady, you took the wrong turning at the crossroads several miles away. Your poor children are exhausted. Jump in, I will take you back.'

It was the first time I had been in a car. I forgot all about the terrifying ordeal at the railing. Riding in this man's motor car was the ultimate experience for me, until I fell asleep.

'Ellie, wake up, we're here.' My mother's voice broke my slumber.

The car had stopped outside a dilapidated smallholding. The building looked to be low and heavy – half stone, half wood, with very small windows. It was surrounded by a kitchen garden, stables and farmland. Three or four goats were standing around trying to reach the leaves of the trees.

A little old lady stood in the front doorway. She had a round face, and her hair was plaited and wound around her head. Her house smelled strange, and it was very dark inside because of the small windows.

For our supper she gave us goats' milk and homemade bread. The milk tasted oily and leafy: it was disgusting. I asked my mother why it tasted so foul. She said because the goats only eat leaves from the trees, and nothing else.

I decided I did not like this place.

Chapter Four

I do not remember how long we stayed at that place. All I remember is that my father found us and took us home.

At first, Mother was reluctant to go home with my father. They would talk for what felt like hours, walking up and down the fields behind the farmhouse. In the end my father made a promise to marry my mother and to change his ways.

The marriage took place in the village of Sittick. I was there at the ceremony when they took the vows. All I remember was being in the church with the Catholic priest standing in front of the altar. I was hanging on to Mother's skirts. After the ceremony we went back to Father's favourite gasthaus for the celebration.

It didn't worry me that we were going to be with my father again, even though I knew it would be the same as it had been before, with the fighting and arguing. I was so used to it. I was never frightened of my father because he never hurt us children; only my other, because she antagonised him so much.

The next thing I knew was that we were moving again. All our belongings fitted easily onto a cart, and we relocated to a village called Radweg near the main road, which was much nearer to where my father's sisters lived.

Father had four sisters and one brother, who was called Ernst. The eldest sister was called Julia. She was my godmother when I was christened, and was the nicest of them all. Julia, Hanna and Fanny lived at a farmhouse in the village of Knasweg. I was able to get to know them when my family moved to Radweg, which was only a kilometre away from Knasweg.

The farmer had a wife, but that did not stop him sleeping with the sisters. The youngest sister, Mitzi, died in childbirth – with his child. I never had the chance to meet her.

My Aunt Julia had two sons by the farmer. The eldest, Gotfried, was disabled and lived half his life in various institutions. The second child was called Walter, and he was a year or so older than I was. I did like my Aunt Julia, and would often go and visit her in the one room that the farmer allotted to her and her sons.

My father would take every opportunity he could to spend time with his sisters and the farmer, drinking cider and playing cards. He would come home drunk at three in the morning, usually having lost all his money.

My mother hated those sisters with a vengeance, and the feeling was mutual. They would incite Friedrich to such a pitch that he came home accusing Maria of all sorts of things. This would give his sisters enormous pleasure. My mother endured much grief over those sisters of my father.

Once again we were living in a tiny cottage. This one had two rooms, but only one was for the four of us.

The bus stop was much closer, next to the only gasthaus. Not that my father used this particular gasthaus: he preferred his old haunts, his old drinking partners. Mother had thought that moving away from the old village would get him away from his drinking cronies. Sadly, she was wrong – it just took him longer to get there and back.

As before, Mother worked on neighbouring farms to earn money for food. And as before Englbert and I would be locked in at home while she was out at work. Englbert would be dressed in my cast-off dresses. He was always dressed like a girl – we called him Bubi, which means 'Baby boy'. He was always Bubi to us.

Time passes so slowly when you are locked in a room no larger than fourteen by twelve feet for hours on end. The fire in the stove would be left burning, and one day I got hold of a red-hot poker and chased Englbert around the room with it. I was no more than five or six years old, but I should have known better.

Bubi was badly burned with the poker. He wouldn't stop crying, and no one could help us as the door was locked from the outside. Here we were, two lonely little children locked in a room, waiting till their mother returned from the field.

I knew exactly what would happen to me – I would get the spanking of my life. Numb with fear, I hid under the bed when I heard Mother putting the key into the front door.

Bubi was still crying; I was hiding under the bed: she knew immediately that something was wrong.

'Mama, I'm sorry. I didn't mean to hurt Bubi.'

She was already in a bad mood from working so hard in

the field, and all my begging and promising to be good did nothing to soften my mother's heart. I would often be beaten with a stick when I was naughty. If she didn't have a rod or a stick, she would go outside and cut one from a hazel bush, and then she would hit me until she got tired or until the stick broke. While she was beating me I was not allowed to cry. The more I cried, the more she would hit me.

This time it was different. After the expected beating, I watched as my mother put some bread and an apple into a handkerchief. She shoved it towards me. 'Get out of my sight,' she said, and put me out of the door.

Surely she did not mean me to get out of her sight for ever? Yet, as I looked into her face, the anger and rage that I could see frightened me more than any of the beatings I had ever endured at her hand.

I picked up the little bundle that Mother had put together and ran as fast as my little legs could carry me. I did not care where I was going, as long as it was far away from her.

I stopped running when I came to a glade in the woods. The weals on the backs of my legs were hurting. I unwrapped the bundle and ate all of the bread and the apple, I was so hungry.

Exhausted from the running and from the emotion of the whole situation, I fell asleep.

I awoke when a hand touched me, and I opened my eyes to see an old lady standing over me. She had a friendly smile on her wrinkled face.

'Hello,' she said. 'Where have you come from? Where is your mummy?'

I looked at her suspiciously. I had been told never to trust strangers. But this elderly lady had a soft voice and warm eyes. But I could not bring myself to tell her that I had been so naughty and had burned my little brother with a poker.

'What is your name?' she asked gently.

'Ellie,' I said.

The lady took me to her cottage, gave me some warm milk and put me to bed.

When I awoke in the morning she gave me some bread and milk, and put some soothing, smelly salve on my legs.

I stayed with her for two days, and I loved every minute of it. I had never received so much attention in the whole of my life.

It took her two days to find out where I had come from. On the third day she bundled me up and took me back to my mother. Mother thanked the old lady profusely and told her how she and Father had been out looking for me.

I got no hugs or kisses when I returned. Mother never hugged or kissed me. But I guess she was happy to see me. 'Don't run away again,' she said to me. But that just confused me. Why had she told me get out if she didn't mean it?

She had thought I would only go to the end of the road and then sneak back in when it was dark. But I didn't. I had kept going, out of sheer stubbornness.

Chapter Five

We were moving again, this time to a large farmhouse, called Bichelbourer (Hilltop Farm). Its name was appropriate because it stood at the top of a steep hill, very close to the village.

The Catholic church stood in the centre of the village, surrounded by five farmhouses. The priory, which resembled a mansion, stood next to a gasthaus-cum-farm. The village also had two cabinet makers and a very fine schoolhouse.

The farmhouse that we moved into was two storeys high, although only the ground floor was fit to live in.

It was the first time we had ever had more than one room to live in: now we had two large rooms to spread ourselves out in.

The top floor was uninhabitable and therefore empty. It had large rooms with broken floorboards and no windows. There was a balcony that ran all the way around the house, where Mother used to hang the washing. It was a great place to play.

To me, the house was quite frightening. To the left of the

kitchen stood a six-foot table which had lots of candle burns on it. I was told that table had been used to lay out the dead. The hallway was enormous, with loose floorboards, and every time we walked by that six foot table, it would jump.

The cellar was just as bad. The steps were to the right as we stepped out of the kitchen door. There were thirteen steps. The left side of the cellar was for storing coal, and the right was for fruit and vegetables.

The cellar was like an underground tunnel, and the only light would be a candle. Very often the candle would go out, and I would be left standing in the dark, petrified. I hated going down to that dark hole.

My mother was given this accommodation on the understanding that she would work five days a week on the estate. The estate belonged to Count Goess, but it was managed by Mr and Mrs Kogler, who had five sons. Mr Kogler was a hard taskmaster. Mother was not allowed to have any time off, even if one of us children was ill. She just had to leave us at the house.

Count and Countess Goess lived in a castle at the foot of the mountain. Surrounding the castle were several buildings, as well as Mr Kogler's large farmhouse and stables. There was also a lake where the Count's family would go swimming.

The Count and Countess had thirteen children. The youngest girl, Emma, went to school with me. I started school when I was six and a half, but for some reason I was put back a year.

I was a very shy, timid child, easily frightened of adults. I would hide in corners. Mother constantly told me I was stupid, good for nothing. I became clumsy, dropping things and very often breaking them. Then Mother would get the stick off the wardrobe. 'You stupid girl! Why can't you be more careful?' I was too frightened to even think straight.

There were several buildings around our farmhouse. Two cottages were inhabited by large families. There were also two stables: one was very large and held between twenty and thirty cows and horses. The other one was for pigs, but it was empty.

Mother obtained permission to use the pigsty, so we got a goat and some chickens.

There were places up the mountain where the trees had been felled and new grass was growing, so mother obtained permission for our goat to be taken up there for grazing. Every morning at six o'clock I had to get up out of my warm bed and take the goat up the mountain for two hours before going to school.

I had to be at school by eight o'clock in the morning. If I was late I was given detention and a hundred lines ('I must not be late for school'). If I was given a detention at school, I received a beating from my mother; it was a vicious circle.

Chapter Six

It was 1938. Everything was changing in the village. The Nazis were becoming increasingly active. One of the best farms in the village was taken over by a German family. We never did find out where the rightful owner had been sent to.

The mood in the village was frightened and dejected. My mother told us children not to say anything that might upset the Germans because we would be truly punished and Mother and Father would be sent away, or even shot. My mother hated the Germans wholeheartedly.

Herr Pothofe, the new owner of the farm, paraded boldly on his horse and cart. He would sing at the top of his voice as he drove through the village, 'We are marching to England!'

There were things going on that we children did not understand. One day we were told to go and stay with our neighbour. My father ran down the hill to fetch the cabinet maker's wife, who was the midwife of the village. She was a very large lady: my father had to physically push her up the hill. I can still see her in my mind's eye. It was such a comical situation – my father pushing and the woman panting and out of breath until they got to the top of the hill to our farmhouse.

It was hours before we were allowed to go home, but when we did finally go home we had a little brother.

Pouby only lived for three months. He was a beautiful baby with lots of black hair. Why he died I never was told. I remember my mother dressing him in white stockings and a white nightshirt. For three nights we had to sit up all night keeping watch over him.

When it came to putting him in his coffin, the joiner had made it too small. Pouby's little body was bent up, and it did not fit. My mother went into a frantic fit of fury. To think of her little baby being bent up in that way was unthinkably cruel to her. The little white coffin had to be taken back and remade.

On the day of the funeral, my father stood by our kitchen window, looking out but not seeing anything. All he wanted was to get away as soon as possible and go to his favourite drinking hole. That is exactly what he did.

After two days he came home so drunk that my mother refused to let him in. He slept where he fell, under the rain gutter in front of our farmhouse. It was raining hard. He was so drunk he never woke up once. In the morning Mother brought him indoors and dried him off with warm towels.

A year later, on 7th October 1939, my brother Fritzi was born. He had black curly hair and was the cutest little baby I had ever seen.

My mother loved him more than everything and everyone else in the whole world: he was her darling. He was not allowed to get hurt: if he did, I was seen to be the one responsible for it, and I would be beaten with the cane till my back would bleed. Yet for some reason I was never jealous of all the love my mother showered on my little brother, because I loved him too.

I was seven years old at that time and my brother Englbert was four. As I was older than my two little brothers, I was like a little mother to them while Mother went to work. I learned to keep the house clean and do the cooking while Mother was working. She would come home from the fields so tired that she would fall asleep on the homemade bench in the kitchen.

While Mother was sleeping, we children were not allowed to make any noise. We would be as quiet as church mice. I was never quite sure what sort of a mood she would be in when she awoke.

Not only was I responsible for my brothers, but I also had to take care of the animals. We had two goats and a dozen chickens. When I took the goats up the mountain for two hours before school, I had to take them high up so they could feed on the new shoots and grasses.

My neighbour, Luzi, would come with me, as her family owned two goats. We were never given any shoes to wear in the summer. First thing in the morning it was very cold on our feet, and we would be walking on painful thorns. Mother would call me from the valley below. 'Ellie,' she would shout, 'bring the goats down. It's time for school.'

I hated those goats. Some days they just would not feed: they would stand there and turn their scrawny necks round and round in a circle, so when it was time to take them home their bellies were empty. There was nothing I could do to make them eat.

I knew I would get a beating. As soon as Mother saw the goats with their empty bellies, out came the cane. After the beating, I was told to take them back up the mountain until dark. Many a time I missed school – sometimes for several days at a time.

One of the things I hated most was killing things, and my mother knew it. One day she ordered me to kill a chicken for our dinner.

We had a chopping block out in the woodshed. I laid the chicken's neck on the chopping block. My left hand was holding its feet, and in my right hand I held a small axe. I swung the axe and the chicken's head fell to the ground. I could not hold on to the chicken: it fluttered so violently in my hand, I let it go. It flew thirty metres into the air and landed in a pear tree.

Tears were running down my face. I hated my mother for making me do this.

In 1940 my father received his call-up papers to join the German Air Force. He looked very handsome in his uniform, six feet tall with his black curly hair, big brown eyes and toothbrush moustache.

After he left, life was quieter and Mother was easier to live with. There was no more horrendous fighting every weekend when Mother would be beaten up and dragged out onto the lawn by her long hair just because she wanted some housekeeping money to pay for food and clothing for us children.

Mother's dresses were patched so many times it was

impossible to tell where the original material started or ended. My brother Englbert wore my cast-off dresses until he was six years old. Only Fritzi had new things to wear.

I was very much a tomboy, climbing trees and playing football with the boys. My dresses were often torn, and Mother would wait with her cane in her hands to dish out my punishment. If she did not have time at that precise moment she would make me wait all day if necessary, but she always remembered to carry out the punishment. Sometimes it was a beating; at other times she would make me kneel on the hard wooden floor in the bedroom, holding a book over my head while she would lie in bed, watching me. It seemed like hours before she would let me get up and go to my bed.

Chapter Seven

Our neighbour, Mrs Bibal, lived very close to our farmhouse: only a dirt road separated our house from her cottage. Her cottage had only one room for the family's use; the rest was derelict and unsafe. We never saw much of her husband. I could never understand how a woman so ugly could have married a handsome man like Mr Bibal. All of us children were frightened of her – she looked like a witch, and always wore a scarf that was tied under her chin. She had six children, and they all lived in that one room.

Her cottage held a great fascination for us because there was a grapevine growing along one of the walls. It harvested very sweet and tasty grapes. It was hard to resist the temptation to steal into her garden and pick them. But she was never away from her front door for long enough.

Every year she had a new baby. I wanted to know where her babies came from. I was told that there was a deep pond up in the mountain where they would fish them out. I was so intrigued I wanted to see this pond for myself.

Another neighbour lived in a two-roomed cottage fifty metres to the west. Between our farmhouse and their cottage stood the stables and a large pear tree. Mr Spiss and his wife had seven children. Luzi, who was about my age, was the eldest girl. She was the one who would walk up the mountain with me every day to herd the goats.

We would find ways to entertain ourselves to relieve the boredom of grazing those goats every day. We would have tremendous fun swinging from tree to tree, until the branches broke and sometimes we would injure ourselves. While we were playing, we often forgot about our goats, which were wandering off to better pastures.

Panic stricken, we would search the mountainside, and all the while the goats were making their way home. We would find them standing outside the stable, waiting to be let in. On their way down from the mountain they would have a good feed on the luscious crops the farmers were growing, causing extensive damage to the fields.

Mother would be there waiting for me. I would always receive my punishment. Often I would go to school in the mornings with sausage-like weals on my legs and back from the beatings I received. I can understand Mother's frustration – she would have to compensate the farmer for the loss of his crops.

Our farm was called Hilltop Farm. The view from Hilltop Farm was spectacular: we could see the next town seven kilometres away, and all the surrounding mountains and villages. When the bombs started to fall, we saw the railway station being blown to pieces, and farm workers being shot at in the fields. All we could do was stand and stare.

In the hills, the freedom fighters (or the partisans, as they were called) would roam the mountains. At night we could hear them outside our farmhouse looking to steal anything they could get their hands on. Mother always made sure the house was securely locked up before going to bed. But the house was old, and there were many ways that someone could break in if they wanted to.

Our henhouse was raided many times. It was so frightening to listen to the loud whispering of the raiders. We would not go to sleep until they had gone.

Our goat did not yield any milk in winter so we had to go and fetch some. The depot where all the farmers from all the villages unloaded their milk was a kilometre out of the village. Frau Maier, who owned the gasthaus, was in charge of the distribution.

I did not have to graze the goat in winter; instead, every morning before going to school I had to fetch the milk in a billycan. The sun came up like a red balloon and the temperature was twenty degrees below. Icicles would form on my hair, and by the time I got home I would be crying from the pain in my hands and feet. I had no time to warm up: school started at eight and finished at midday. I didn't dare arrive late: I had no desire to stay behind and write lines, and then to receive the subsequent beating from my mother.

Our food supply would run out in early spring. All the crops we had gathered in the autumn would run out. All we would have left were some potatoes, and they would be wrinkled and sprouting.

Many times we went to bed hungry. It is hard to go to sleep with an empty belly. Often we just had some boiled potatoes and a cup of coffee for our evening meal.

By late May even the potatoes ran out.

One night in early June, Mother woke me in the middle of the night. The leaves were rustling in the trees and the sky was as black as your hat; there was no moon at all. Mother did not want to be seen. We walked half a mile until we came to a field where the early potatoes were growing. Mother pulled the plants by the roots and I gathered the potatoes into a basket. The night was cold and eerie. I was half asleep and just wanted to be back in my bed. At other times, if she had the money, Mother would send me to buy potatoes from one of the local farmers.

Spring was also an exciting time, as it was when our pregnant goats would give birth to their kids – very often they had twins – and the baby chicks would begin to hatch.

Mother was able to acquire some land, so we planted our own vegetables, beans and potatoes. Hay had to be gathered for the winter to feed the goats. And I had to look after the house, my two little brothers and the animals. It was hard work. I often had to miss school, sometimes for a couple of weeks at a time.

I dreaded going to school because I knew I would never be able to catch up with my lessons. At the end of summer term, the only A grade that I ever received was for singing.

The Countess, who was my godmother when I took my first Holy Communion, always gave me one shilling and told me to do better.

Chapter Eight

Mother was working in the fields for Mr Kogler when I went running to fetch her. Englbert, who was now five, had jumped off a fence and landed on some two-inch nails, which had gone straight through his foot. It took several tugs to pull them out. He was a fat little boy and it was heavy going for me to get him up the hill to our farmhouse.

But Mr Kogler was adamant that Mother had to get back to the fields: it was harvest time and a storm was about to break. I had to manage as best I could with the injured little boy and baby Fritzi. I was only eight years old myself.

The next day mother stayed home. The only doctor nearby was in the town of Feldkirchen seven kilometres away. Mother was about to leave when Mr Kogler came for her to go to work. Mother wouldn't let Mr Kogler into our house. She locked all the doors and closed all the curtains so he could not see us. But he was persistent and angry; he jumped up at our window, which was open at the time, shouting and demanding that Mother go back to work immediately. If the window had been any bigger I think he would have jumped through it, he was so angry. But Mother stood her ground, and after Mr Kogler gave up and went away she went to fetch the doctor.

We were never given any shoes in the summer. Everywhere we went, we went in bare feet. Mother sent Englbert and me to a farm in the village of Nassweg to herd cattle for the two months of school holidays. For that we were promised some boots for the winter.

As soon as I saw the miserable face of the farmer's wife, I knew I was going to be unhappy staying there.

Our bed was in a small chamber off the kitchen. It was cold and damp, and we only had a thin blanket each.

In the morning we were given some bread and coffee before we took the cattle out onto the marshes to graze. We had to circle the marshes at all times so they would not stray onto neighbouring farm lands.

It was hard on our poor feet. The ground was full of thistles and brambles. Our bare feet were often so cold that we stood in the cows' wee because it was warm.

If there was a storm, lightning would strike the ground and the cows would raise their tails in the air and bolt in all directions. It was a nightmare to round them up again.

We were so tired by the end of the day that we could barely keep our eyes open to eat the leftovers that would be our evening meal. But before we could go to sleep we had to pick out all the thorns and thistles from our poor feet.

These two months were the longest months of our lives. I was so thankful when it was time to go home to our mother.

But we didn't get our new boots; the boots we were given were old and worn. Mother was furious that we had been cheated this way and went storming off to confront the farmer's wife. I don't remember whether or not we got our boots in the end.

September - and back to school. We had religious lessons twice a week on Mondays and Fridays. Father Tremelsberger would teach us all about Jesus and his followers. If I began to lose concentration, he would step off his podium, pick up his heavy Bible and slam it down on top of my head. He would often beat us with a cane – six strokes on our outstretched fingers.

Father Tremelsberger was a dominant force in our village and the villages around us. We had to go to church at least twice a week. On Sundays, even if it was cold, we had to go to church. Mother would wrap our feet in old rags as we had no shoes to wear.

The offering box would be passed from person to person. And the sexton would cruelly ram the box into our ribs. No matter how poor we were, we had to find some money to take to church on a Sunday.

Everyone in the village had to go to confession; therefore the Father knew everyone's secrets. I believe that is how he controlled the people for miles around. Mother had told us stories of priests blackmailing people into giving the church their possessions, and even land and houses. Poor, innocent people were frightened out of their possessions, and for that they were promised that they would go to heaven when they died.

Father Tremelsberger thought I was an unruly child so he sent me to a convent for one week to reform my character. The nuns made us get up at five in the morning to go to chapel, where we had to kneel on the hard stone floor for an hour. Breakfast was a measly portion of bread and dripping with coffee. After that we were put to the hard work of cleaning floors and dormitories.

After lunch there were more religious lessons, then Mass and more prayer. I was glad to get out of there.

And to think I had wanted to be a nun.

In the autumn, we gathered vegetables and fruit for the winter. It was all stored in our cellar – that dark hole that I dreaded so much to enter.

I was sent to different farmers to help with potato picking, for which we were given one hundredweight of potatoes. The same went for apples, cabbages and carrots. Everything went into the cellar.

When all that was finished I was sent to my aunt's farm, where every day after school I had to help with the weekly washing. The heavy linen sheets had to be taken out into the courtyard to the running water trough for rinsing. I was a very skinny little nine-year-old and the work was very heavy, so my arms would ache every evening when I got home.

My aunt's husband was a slimy, dirty man. If he was nearby when I happened to bend over to pick up a basket of washing, he was quick to put his hand up my crotch – but only if his wife was not around. I was too frightened to tell my mother because I was bringing home extra meat and flour that we so desperately needed. I just had to be more careful and keep out of his way.

Autumn was a time for picking blueberries, which grew in abundance if you knew where to look. Mother knew all the places in the mountain. High up she would take us, with lots of containers and baskets to put them in. The next day she would take them into the town of Feldkirchen and sell them for good money.

But one Sunday we were going out without any baskets. We were also going in a different direction.

We followed Mother through the village and across a farm down to the main road, past the gasthaus where my school friend Gerta Maier and her family lived and where I collected our milk from the depot every morning. Then we crossed the main road and passed the small cottage where we used to live before we moved to the farmhouse in the village of Radweg.

Mother led us into a forest to which I had never been before. We walked for a very long time. I thought maybe we were looking for mushrooms, but there were no mushrooms. The forest was becoming very dense. When she found a spot to her liking, she stopped. 'Right,' she said. 'Ellie, I want you to look after your two brothers while I'm gone. I won't be long. Do not move from this spot. Do you hear me, Ellie?'

I said, 'Yes, Mama,' and then she disappeared and was gone.

It was quite dark in those woods: we could barely see the sky. Mother had left us no food or drink so initially I wasn't unduly alarmed, but as it grew later and later I began to get quite nervous. I also knew that many undesirable foreigners were stalking through our land. What if one of them were to walk in our direction?

Fritzi was still a baby and was starting to whimper for his mama – he was, after all, the darling of her life. But there was no sign of her.

We were there in that dense forest all afternoon and it was beginning to get dark. I prayed to God that Mother would come soon – I was getting very frightened. I honestly thought she had abandoned us forever.

When she finally did show up, she never told us where she had been.

That experience stayed in my mind for many years: I would dream that mother would abandon us and never come back.

When the snow started to fall, that was the most magical time. In the weeks leading up to Christmas Mother would be busy knitting jumpers, stockings, gloves and socks as Christmas presents for us children. On Christmas Eve, the three of us were sent to evening Mass at church. Mother would say, 'By the time you children get home from church, Father Christmas will have come with all the presents, but only if you are good.' It was a wonderful and exciting time for us.

As we walked into our house, we would see the tree, lit up with small candles pegged to the branches, lots of homemade biscuits cut out like stars or animals, sweets wrapped in silver paper and lots of angel hair draped across the branches.

In Austria it is the custom to open presents on Christmas Eve rather than Christmas day. There were no toys in our parcels, which were wrapped in brown paper; no, Mother could not afford such luxuries.

Only once in my life did Mother buy me a doll. I think I must have been about nine or ten. It was when she had to carry me on her back for seven kilometres to Feldkirchen to the doctor. I had a tetanus infection in my foot; the doctor had to cut my foot to drain the pus while Mother was watching, and it made her feel very sorry for me. So she bought me the doll.

The doll's head was made out of papier mâché, it had yellow synthetic hair, and the body was made of white linen. Sadly, it did not last long. I tried to comb the hair but it all came out in my hand and became bald very quickly. I wasn't a girl for dolls very much; I was more of a tomboy, always climbing trees and playing football with the boys. I was the fastest runner at school.

Chapter Nine

Spring 1942. Mother was always working for different farmers, mending clothes or in the field. For that she would be paid in kind – mainly with bread, milk or flour. This time she was paid with a live pig, or rather piglet. It was so tiny it fitted into the palm of her hand. She had to feed it with a baby's bottle, and it slept in a shoe box next to the stove. It was pink and silky and we all loved it.

This piglet was the thirteenth of a litter; it would have been thrown out if it weren't for my mother's intervention. It had only just been born, but it was thriving with mother's loving help. It grew very fast and followed my mother's every step, like an adoring puppy.

It was unthinkable to think that in the autumn it would have to be slaughtered.

That spring was also a time when people and disabled children started to disappear. Many Austrians became fervent Nazis; we had to be very careful who we spoke to. One word out of place and you could be taken away, never to be seen again.

We didn't know about the concentration camps, then. All

we knew was that people just disappeared. Your best friend could turn out to be your enemy and betray you.

Our neighbours, the Spiss family with the seven children, were very well looked after because they sported the Nazi flag. Our mother, a very outspoken woman, had to curb her tongue, and she told us children to do likewise.

The spring grasses and flowers were sprouting through the ground and it was time to take our goats up into the mountain for grazing again.

Luzi, her brother Simon and I always went around together. (My brothers were still too small to climb the mountain.) We knew all the best places, where the trees had been felled the previous year and where the new grass was growing in abundance. But we also knew the best places to play, and where we could climb treehouses that the gamekeeper had built so he could watch over the deer and pheasants. Many times he chased us from open spaces where young saplings were growing – the goats loved to eat these new shoots. We had to move our goats from one open space to another to make sure their bellies were full by the time it was time to take them home.

But we would also play in places where there was hardly anything for the goats to eat. They would stand around, twisting their silly necks around in circles. I hated those goats: they got me into so much trouble. I received more beatings from my mother over these goats than because of anything else.

On one occasion we stumbled into an area of forest where we found a cave. Above the cave the rock had formed in a similar shape to a throne. It was the seat that had us children looking in wonder: it looked as though it had the indentation of a woman's bottom. An indentation of a very large woman – in fact, a giant.

This place was hidden away and we only found it by accident. When we told our mother what we had discovered, she told us a lovely story of a giant woman who used to sit on that rock. She was so large and heavy that she made the indentation in the rock, like you would on wet sand by the seaside. Then she would walk down the mountain into the valley below, gather a horse and plough, including the farmer, into her apron, and carry them up to her cave, where she would toy with them. It was a lovely story, and we believed it.

If my mother did not have time to do the shopping, she would send me into the town of Feldkirchen instead. On one occasion, Luzi Spiss, her sister Mitzi and her brother Simon came along too. On the way we met a group of children going the opposite way. These children were extremely aggressive. A fight broke out and stones were thrown, although fortunately they did not hit any target. But when I threw just one stone it happened to hit a target – one of the boys from the other group. The boy began to scream blue murder and threatened to send his father after us. We ran like hell till there was no breath left in us. We reached the town and were very grateful that no one was chasing us.

Our shopping was completed and we were ready to go home. Luzi had some money left over. We passed a toy shop and there, in the window, was a toy aeroplane. It was a bomber like a Spitfire, and came with sulphur capsules so that when you dropped the bomber it made a bang.

On the long walk home we all took turns playing with this aeroplane. In the end, Luzi became tired of it and she gave it to me. She genuinely gave me the toy, but when we got home her mother wanted to know where her change was from the money she had given to Luzi for the shopping. Luzi told her mother that she had bought a toy aeroplane.

'So where is your toy aeroplane?' Mrs Spiss said to Luzi.

'On the way home, Ellie stole it,' Luzi said to her mother.

All hell broke loose. Mrs Spiss came running over to our house, shouting accusations that I was a thief.

Stealing and lying were things my mother did not tolerate. If we took a slice of bread and without telling her, that was stealing. If we were honest and told her, that was fine; otherwise it was stealing.

Mother did not even ask me what had really happened on our journey home from town. She just reached for the cane, which was always on top of our wardrobe, and started to hit me. Blow after blow – she just didn't stop. Between shrieks of pain I tried to tell her that I had not stolen that stupid toy, but she wouldn't listen. She beat me so badly I almost felt faint.

I finally managed to tear myself away from her, and I ran, and I just couldn't stop running. It was getting quite dark by then. I ran through fields and pastures, jumped over fences and ran through streams until I came to a very large haystack. I climbed right to the top of that haystack. I was still crying from the beating I received, but most of all from the injustice of it. I was so deeply hurt I thought I could never forgive her. At that moment I hated my mother for what she had done to me.

I was shivering violently. I wrapped my arms around myself and hid in the hay.

I woke up during the night and could hear voices below. Men's voices. I was petrified. What if they felt cold and climbed the haystack too? I would certainly be raped. I was trembling with fear.

I thanked God when at dawn the men left.

In the meantime, my mother was actually worried about me. She looked for me all night. She went as far as to my aunt's house, five kilometres from our home.

I the morning, I crawled out of the haystack feeling very sore and hungry. I had no idea what to do next. I was frightened to go home, frightened of my mother, knowing she could bear a grudge and might well have carried on with the beating from the night before. I began to wander across the field, slowing heading towards home.

It was lunchtime when I saw mother in the distance. I sat there in the high grass just looking over towards her. I sat there for a long time, too frightened to go near her.

Mother had two goats out with her that were grazing beside her, when she saw me. She beckoned me to come to her, but I was reluctant. However, hunger soon prevailed so I slowly crept closer until I stood before her.

I thought she would hug me and tell me she had punished me wrongly, but not my mother: there was no regret for beating me so severely, no softness to show me that she was sorry for beating a nine-year old so badly. All she said was, 'You deserved it.'

But she did fall out with the Spiss family. And for a long time I would not forgive Luzi Spiss for her betrayal.

Chapter Ten

The war was in full swing. We could hear the bombs falling for miles around. Undesirables would roam around the countryside, especially at night. Children who were deaf, dumb, deformed or disabled in any way would be taken away. Hitler wanted only healthy people. These children were taken to Klagenfurt main hospital and given a lethal injection to put them to sleep forever.

Many people would hide their children in lofts or cellars to save their lives. One man, who happened to be a friend of my mother's, was known to be one of those who did the injecting. After the war, he was convicted of killing many children.

Our piglet had grown big and fat. Mother fed it on mashed potatoes and corn mash. November was the usual time to slaughter, and by law we should give half of the pig to the Hitler regime. However, Mother had no intention of doing such a thing. So the pig had to be killed at night when there was no one around to see.

First she gave the pig some grain in a bowl. While the pig was happily munching on the grain, she knocked him unconscious with a large hammer and then stabbed him in the throat to let all the blood out. At the same time she had to catch the blood in a bucket, but she couldn't do both at the same time. 'Ellie,' she shouted, 'come and hold the bucket.' But I had done a runner. I did not care if I got a real beating for this: I could not watch while she killed our beloved pig.

All through the night she worked. She put the carcass into a tin bath of hot water and, with the help of chains, rubbed all the bristles off. The pig was hung on a hook and carved up into small sections. These sections were then put into a large barrel with garlic and salt for six weeks to preserve them. Then it had to be smoked for another six weeks.

That pig gave us food for several months. With the vegetables we had stored in our cellar, we had food until early spring. But from May onwards, until the new vegetables grew, we were very hungry. Often we had to go to bed with just a slice of bread and coffee, or salted boiled potatoes.

In the spring, Mother would purchase day-old chicks, some for laying eggs and others for eating, but of course they had to grow first. In the summer we would lose a lot of chickens: foxes would come down from the mountain rocks where they had their lair.

My father, Friedrich Rohm, was stationed in Paris. He was in the German RAF. One day, in the summer of 1943, Mother made up her mind to travel all the way to Paris to see him.

But, of course, I did not know that: all she said was that she was going away for a day or so and I was to look after the boys and the animals.

We all accompanied her to the train station in Feldkirchen seven kilometres away and said our goodbyes. 'Ellie,' she said, 'look after the boys, and if you get stuck and need help, go to Mrs Spiss.' She kissed us and stepped on to the train. 'I'll only be a couple of days,' she called from the open window of the train.

But she wasn't.

I hated being alone with my two little brothers in that large, weird house. At night we would hear the house creaking and the wind howling through the upper floorboards. Everyone said the house was haunted. Little Fritzi would not sleep by himself, so we all huddled in one bed to sleep, we were so frightened.

Ideas of what to cook and feed us with ran out after a few days. I had no choice but to go to my next door neighbour who had seven children of her own. All our food was running short.

Baby Fritzi was fretting for his mama. He was so spoiled by her; he was the darling boy. I had the goats and the chickens to feed and I had to clean and cook for all of us. I was not even eleven years old.

Englbert and Fritzi were fast asleep one night when I heard low whispers outside our bedroom window. I knew the partisans were back, creeping around the farmhouse. I was numb with fear. Would they try and break in? There was nothing for them to steal; we were very poor – except for the animals, of course.

After a week of being home alone, we walked the seven kilometres to the railway station to see if Mother was on the train. There was only one train running each day, in the late evening. But mother was not on that train. I consoled

Englbert and Fritzi and told them, 'She'll come tomorrow.'

Tomorrow came and went, but Mother did not arrive back. Every evening from then on we walked to the train station, but Mother still did not return. Although Mother was very cruel to me and Englbert, we still loved her.

I was very worried but I could not show it. I did not want to frighten the boys if mother had indeed abandoned us. I had heard of people being taken away by the Nazis. At night I cried myself to sleep.

After two weeks, Mother came back. There was no explanation. She didn't even ask how I had coped. Nothing. She didn't tell me where she had been until some months later when she described how she had nearly been killed when the train she was on was riddled with bullets from an enemy plane and lots of passengers were killed.

For the rest of that summer I was sent to another farmer to herd their cattle in all weathers, still without shoes.

Chapter Eleven

In spring 1944 there began to be a lot of activity in the other half of our farmhouse. Carpenters were preparing bunk beds, and our hall was divided so we would not go through to the back. Instead, we had to go around the house to get to the stables where our animals were housed.

The village was overrun with German guards and officers. They were looking for suitable accommodation for their indefinite stay.

And then they arrived, ten English prisoners of war were billeted in our farmhouse. They were assigned to work in the forest as loggers. Every day, German officers would come early in the morning to take them up into the mountains to log trees. And every evening they would bring them back.

The English POWs did their own cooking and washing, and we benefited greatly. The Red Cross would send them food parcels and they had plenty of food, and gave us biscuits and chocolates. Above all, they loved my baby brother Fritzi: that little boy would be passed from one pair of arms to another.

The only downside of this was that my mother had to

cook for one of the German officers. I was very worried because mother hated the Germans with a passion. One wrong word and she would be taken away into a concentration camp. It was hard for her to keep a civil tongue in her mouth.

It was very unfortunate that Mother was ordered to cook for a German officer. Austrian food is very different from German food.

Mother tried very hard to please the man, offering him different dishes.

'What is this? I cannot eat this rubbish,' the German officer would say. 'Can't you cook?'

Mother was hot-tempered by nature, and she hated the Germans with a passion. I remember seeing her standing by the kitchen stove with a knife in her hand. She turned to face him and threw the knife at him. It was very lucky for her that she missed.

We were very lucky to be living in the country. The Post Office was seven kilometres away, so the German officer's report took much longer to get through than it would have from the town.

We were on tenterhooks for weeks. We waited and waited for the Gestapo to come and arrest my mother, but no one came. The war was going badly so everything was held up in the city.

Life went on as normally as possible. I still had to get up at six in the morning to take the goats up the mountain to feed for two hours. There was a fox family in one of the caves, and they would come down to our farm and steal our chickens. One day we lost eleven chickens – the foxes just killed them and left them lying around the courtyard.

Mother was very upset. We had no freezer in those days to store the meat. Every year the foxes would kill our chickens.

That year we also lost one of our goats. The neighbouring farmer's cow stabbed it with her long horn, right through the goat's stomach.

The school summer holidays came around once more. This time I was sent to my Aunty Angie's farm to herd her cattle.

Every day I had to take my aunt and uncle's cows to different grazing fields. One day my uncle told me to take the cattle to the furthest grazing field, which was a kilometre away from the village. It was a cold, overcast day. A fast-flowing river surrounded the field; I had to keep the cattle away from it so that they would not accidentally fall in and be swept away.

As I was nearing the edge of the river where the hazel bushes grew, I saw a man standing there. His long coat was open and his trousers were unbuttoned. He was exposing himself and quite openly playing with his genitals. I was brought up in the country so I was aware of such things. Also, my uncle was a very crude man and would often talk of sex and exposures.

But I was all alone in this vast grazing field. There was no one around except me and the cows. I thought of running back to my aunt's but I could not leave the animals to wander off and get lost – my uncle would kill me. After a while the man must have grown tired of standing there and disappeared into the bushes.

I was very shaken when I got back and told my half-brother Val. He, too, was quite shocked.

My mother had found some material in the attic of the

farmhouse we were living in. It must have belonged to the family that lived upstairs. It was crushed velvet in a deep burgundy colour. She made me a dress from it. I loved that dress. I wore it to the village fete, which was where I learned to dance the waltz and the polka. Although I was only eleven I was allowed to drink schnapps and got quite tipsy. The village festival went on for two days. The villagers were falling over drunk all over the place.

I loved it when Aunty Angie would say to me, 'Ellie, go get the horses from the field.' I could ride the horses back to the stables. It was just the early mornings I didn't like. My aunt would rap the windows from outside and shout, 'Ellie, get up! Ellie, get up!'

My uncle and I had to get up very early one morning. It was a two-and-a-half hour climb to the Alps. The trail was very steep, and the sun was hot on our backs.

Halfway up we could see that the growth of some of the trees had been stunted. The view all around us was quite beautiful. We settled down for a rest and to eat the lunch which my aunt had prepared for us. My uncle was drinking cider from a flask. He was a coarse, rude man, and I knew he was fond of groping women. I always felt very uncomfortable whenever I was anywhere near him. I had not been able to come up with a good excuse not to take this trip up to the mountain. What could I say? That I was afraid of him? All they would have said to me was, 'Don't be stupid – it's your uncle.'

But I had an uneasy feeling just the same. And it turned out I was right to be on my guard. After my uncle had drunk his fill, he started to touch me. First he put his hand on my chest, then he gradually manoeuvred his whole body on top of me. Although I was tall for my eleven years, I could not equal the strength of a fully grown man. As his hand was groping my thigh, I was getting very frightened indeed. I was pleading for him to get off of me. I was frantically trying to fight him off; I did not want to be raped by my uncle.

Fortunately, my crying and screaming brought him to his senses. My dress was undone, my hair was dishevelled, and I was wet with sweat and shaking all over. Was I glad to get down from that mountain and away from him.

I couldn't tell anybody what had happened to me. What could I say? No one would have believed me anyway, and they would have said that I was a stupid little girl who told a load of lies.

I prayed that my mother would come to visit so that I could go home with her. My uncle might just try it again when he had been drinking.

I'm glad to say I can't remember ever going to visit my aunt and uncle again after that summer.

Chapter Twelve

The war was going very badly for the Germans. It was early in the spring of 1945 and the British prisoners of war were packing up ready to leave our farmhouse. In their place, we received refugees from the capital of Klagenfurt. A family moved into the upstairs room of our house. The mother with her two daughters had been bombed out and had nowhere else to go. They were proper townspeople, all posh and la-di-dah, and they kept themselves to themselves.

Half of our stable was rebuilt to accommodate more bunk beds. Instead of more British prisoners of war, some Russians arrived. It felt as though we were overrun with Russian soldiers. Some had to be carried: they were all very sick, injured, lice-ridden men. They brought with them horses and donkeys which they killed for meat, as food was so scarce. Mother made sure we children were kept away from these frightful-looking men.

Once the Russians invaded our land, it was said that a lot of young women were being raped all over the country. No one felt safe walking alone in the field or the woods.

The Russian prisoners of war were treating themselves with herbs from Mother's garden. Half a kilometre away from our house was a small pond where we children used to swim in the summer, but the Russians thought that the mud at the bottom of this pond had healing powers. They took large canisters to collect the mud, then it was heated to boiling point. The heated mud was then applied to their whole bodies.

I cannot remember how long these Russian soldiers stayed at our farmhouse because I was once again sent to herd cows on a farm.

In September 1945 we went back to school. By then the Russians had departed, but the British army was moving in. Our schoolhouse was taken over by British soldiers so we had to have our lessons in the school gardens.

We children were given lots of chocolates by these men. I would always save my chocolates for my mother and my two brothers.

Having all these men around who were starved of female company was quite a problem. It would be easy to be lured as they would beckon young ladies to come to them.

My mother rented a meadow from Count Goess. After mowing we would take our goats there to graze. It was a hilly meadow. After school one day, I was watching our goats from the top of this hill when one of the British soldiers came creeping along the bushes at the bottom, beckoning me to come down to him. I was almost thirteen years old, and I knew very well what he wanted. He was showing me chocolates and biscuits that he had brought with him to entice me down to him.

I was very nervous. What if my mother came along? I was more frightened of my mother than I was of that man.

I must say he was very persistent in his sign language: none of the British soldiers spoke any German.

Any girl caught going out with one of the soldiers would have their hair shaved off so the whole village knew of the disgrace. But these soldiers were very persistent and would follow you on an empty road. It was very dangerous for young girls – some were even raped.

Mr Pothofe, the German Nazi farmer who had the best farmhouse and acres and acres of land, was terrified when the British walked into his house, marched him out at gunpoint, gave him a spade and told him to dig his own grave.

Mr Pothofe was so frightened he was crying and whimpering. The whole village was looking on. Only a month earlier he had been shouting, 'We will march towards England!' and, 'Heil Hitler!' Now he was a frightened wreck of a man.

After he had dug the hole he was told, 'It is our latrine you have been digging.'

The whole village was laughing hysterically.

Chapter Thirteen

The farmhouse we lived in was very old, and every so often the chimney caught fire. Everyone had to help carry water buckets to the top of the house to put it out. To try and prevent this, once a month the chimney sweep would come and climb into the enormous chimney to sweep it. He was a tall and lanky young man.

But beware should you meet him when walking home alone on a deserted road. He was known for womanising, and was said to rape any skirt he came across that wasn't hanging on a tree, as the saying went. For miles around girls were warned to keep out of his way.

One day I had to do an errand for my mother – to get some milk and butter. I had to walk through woods to the neighbouring farm about half a mile away.

On my way back I was unfortunate enough to meet up with (you guessed it) the chimney sweep. He was standing in my pathway. At first we were just standing there looking at each other. I was working out how I was going to get past him, thinking, 'No way is he going to touch me!' He was bigger than I was but I was quite tall for my age and strong from all the heavy chores my mother made me do.

The path was narrow. On my right was a sheer drop, and to my left the area was densely packed with young fir trees. There was nowhere to run. I had to face him. He tried to wrestle me to the ground. I kicked and scratched and he couldn't get a hold on me. The words kept going through my mind: 'No one is going to rape me.' And anyway, my mother would kill me.

By the time I had fought him off I was as black as the chimney sweep.

The first thing I had to do was clean myself up: I had to find a stream. I had to walk a long way to find a stream. My arms were so black, the only way I could remove the soot was to rub it off with mud.

By the time I got home, my dress was drying and I had calmed down considerably. Fortunately my mother noticed nothing: I was always dirty anyway, from cleaning the goats and mucking out the pigs.

At Easter 1946 I finished school. I had to find a job - and quick. Mother wanted me to move out. 'I cannot feed you,' she would say. She found me a job helping in the kitchen and the stables with a family named Pingist. Their house stood on the outskirts of our village, right next to the road. Mrs Pingist was heavily pregnant and suffered with extreme back and stomach pains. I liked helping her: she was a very nice, genteel lady.

But Mr Pingist was a different kettle of fish. He was known to be a womaniser. I kept my distance as much as I could. He had a carpenter's workshop at the back of his house as well as a smallholding and two milking cows, a pig and dozens of chickens.

I had to work very hard. In the morning I would help in the kitchen and in the afternoon I would work out in the field.

My bed was made up in the large kitchen. I could never go to sleep until everyone else had gone to bed.

Mr Pingist was in the habit of going shopping for his wife on Saturday afternoons. He would time his excursion so that he would get home very late in the evening. He had to come into the kitchen where I slept. I dreaded Saturdays. After putting his shopping away he would come and sit on my bed. At first he just talked. He told me when the safest time was for having sex so as not to get pregnant. Then he wanted to show me the French kiss. That went on for weeks.

I didn't know what to do or who to tell. I felt frightened and silly at the same time.

But one Saturday night he came home drunk. He wanted more than just to talk. He put his hand on my breasts and said, 'I want to give you a French kiss.' His wife was asleep upstairs in their bedroom; that poor woman was suffering enough – I could not cry out. I tried to push him away but he was six feet tall, plus he was drunk.

I started to cry. I said that I would wake his wife and he would not like that. Eventually he got up from my bed and left the kitchen. The next day nothing was said. But I dreaded Saturday coming round again.

During the following week I saw my mother walking past the house. I stopped her and told her what Mr Pingist was up to on Saturday evenings when he came home from his shopping trips. 'Don't be stupid,' Mother said, 'he is a decent man, and with his wife in the house he wouldn't do such a thing.' And that was that.

Mother was worried that I would lose my job and then she'd have me at home again. I'm sure that was the reason she didn't want to know. I had only been at this job for about two and a half months and jobs weren't exactly falling off the trees. It seemed to me that she wasn't worried about me at all.

The only free time I had was when I went to church on a Sunday. After church the following Sunday I met up with my best friend Gerta Maier. I told her what had been going on and that I had told my mother but she wouldn't believe me.

Ours was a very small village, and anything said spread like wildfire. Gerta told her mother what I had said. Then Gerta's mother told someone else from the village. The ball was rolling and the whole thing got back to my mother.

Mother came storming to the house demanding to speak to Mr Pingist and his wife. I was terrified. Mother always frightened me, but now I was more frightened of Mr Pingist – he wasn't an easy man to be around.

It was horrible. I had to stand there and tell poor Mrs Pingist what her husband had been getting up to on Saturday nights while she was sleeping upstairs.

Of course, I couldn't stay at my job any longer. But I couldn't leave straight away either: I had to give two weeks' notice. They were the longest two weeks of my life. In those two weeks Mr Pingist made my life hell. He made me do the dirtiest jobs, milk the cows at six o'clock in the morning and muck out the pigsty. It was horrendous. I was so exhausted every night when I got to bed. But one thing at least was better: he didn't come into the kitchen at night any more.

I was so glad when the time came to leave that house.

Chapter Fourteen

When my father came home from the war he did not come home to us. Instead he went to his sisters', which my mother hated with a passion. We discovered that my father was staying with his sisters in the next village by a roundabout way.

My mother was furious. She was already cross that I had lost my job, and now this. She went storming off to where the sisters lived with the farmer in the next village. Father had been back from the war for a whole week he and he had not been bothered to come home to his own family.

When mother got there he was so drunk on the farmer's cider he didn't even bother to justify himself.

There was the most terrible argument: Mother accused the sisters of keeping Father for themselves. It wasn't a pleasant homecoming. The fights started all over again; furniture got broken, Mother got beaten up again. Nothing had changed. My father was still the bad-tempered, cruel drunk that he always had been.

Once a year our village held its annual festival. The whole village would go to church in the morning and the priest would lead the congregation all round the village. In the afternoon, a dance floor was erected in a field, and there would also be hot dog stands, shooting galleries and other sideshows. The dancing would go on until two or three o'clock in the morning.

Once I had finished my chores I was allowed to go to the dance, accompanied by my parents. My father was a pain in the neck; he followed me everywhere. I can understand his anguish – I was only fourteen years old. I loved dancing and music. I wasn't interested in boys; as long as I could dance, I was happy.

I remember one boy I met at a dance. He would walk for miles just to come and see me. One night he fell asleep at our kitchen table, he was so tired. I just left him there and went to bed. My mother said, 'You are very cruel to that boy. You do not deserve a decent boy if you carry on like that.'

I wanted to leave home as soon as possible. But the only work I could find was temporary. The advert was in a local paper. An elderly lady wanted temporary help in her villa by the lake. It was the largest lake in our county, called the Woitersee.

My job was to clean the villa from top to bottom. She also had a goat that I had to care for.

Every evening after work I was able to go swimming in the lake. There was also a boathouse that belonged to the villa, and it was surrounded by a large orchard. It was a hot summer and I loved it there.

Because I went swimming every day, even when I had my period, the old lady summoned my mother and asked her whether I was pregnant.

I was confronted by both women. 'Are you pregnant?' they asked in unison.

I looked my mother in the eye. 'No, Mother, I am not.'

The old lady said, 'But you go swimming every day.'

'Have I done something wrong?' I asked. I truly did not know that a lady should not go swimming during her monthly period.

Both women were mightily relieved. I had been brought up a very strict Catholic. I couldn't imagine going with a boy at my age, and what would I tell the priest when I went to confession on Sundays? I think between Mother and the priest they would likely kill me.

The time passed very quickly at the villa. By October the old lady was shutting the whole house and I was out of work once more.

The next job my mother found for me was even shorter.

I was taken to Klagenfurt, the capital town of Korinthia. The lady I was to work for had a photographic shop in the centre of town. She had a three-year old daughter, and her mother also lived with them.

I cleaned and scrubbed the house all day long. I was not allowed to even talk to the little girl: if the child spoke to me I was to ignore her. I was a domestic and therefore treated as such.

The old lady was the most unpleasant woman I had ever come across. My mother was bad enough, but she had nothing on that old lady. Every day was true torture in that household. Two weeks went by and it felt like a year.

One morning I asked for permission to go to the shops. I said I needed some sanitary towels very badly. The old lady said, 'OK but be quick about it. You're here to work, not to run around to the shops.'

I put on my coat and left the house. It had all worked out. I would go to the photographic shop, ask my employer to advance me some money and then leave quietly without the old lady noticing. Well, that was what I had hoped. The previous evening I had packed my few belongings and was ready to go.

But when I got back to the house the old lady had gone into my room and discovered my clothes all packed. She said to me, 'What are you up to, you deceitful child? Were you thinking of running away?'

I was shaking like a leaf but I made myself stand up to her. I said, 'I am going home. I have worked hard and still you treat me so badly.' She grabbed hold of me and pushed me into the bathroom, and then she locked the door. She told me she would keep me locked up till her daughter came home from work. That was lunchtime, and the lady of the house did not come home until six in the evening. But I had made up my mind. I did not care what would happen: I would not stay.

It must have been late afternoon when the doorbell rang. I banged on the bathroom door with my fists to make myself heard. I could hear a woman's voice. It was my mother. She had come to check how I was getting on at my new job and demanded to see me. Mother was none too pleased to find me locked in the bathroom and wanted to know what had been going on. I told her I was being treated badly by this old lady.

Mother said, 'Where are your things? We are leaving.'

The old lady tried to stop us, but to no avail. Was I glad to get out of there!

Mother at the back of our farmhouse

Mother and baby Fritzi. Mother was 38 years old

Fritzi with donkeys

My first Communion, aged 8. 1940

Me aged 13. Behind me is my school house and our village

Mother and Father, 1952

Chapter Fifteen

My next job was again in Klagenfurt. This time it was in a gasthaus. It had ten bedrooms for short-stay guests. I was employed as a kitchen maid/housemaid/chambermaid. In fact, I was a maid for every job there was. I worked from six in the morning until ten at night.

The landlord had a wife who lived in the attic, but the landlord and his mistress ran the business. She was young, aggressive and very hard to please.

First thing in the morning I had to light the stove, then breakfast had to be made for the guests, and then the vegetables had to be prepared for lunch. The ten bedrooms had to be stripped and remade. In the afternoon we had to wash all the bed sheets in the wash house across the courtyard. To rinse the linen we had to carry the heavy baskets across the main road from the gasthaus down to the canal, rinse the sheets and then carry them all the way back to hang them on the line in the garden. We had to do this every day.

At first there two other girls as well as me to do all these chores, but after a few weeks they gave notice and left, until I was the only one left. So I had to do the work of three people day after day. I was only fifteen years old.

My room was in the attic right at the top of the house. One Saturday I went to a dance and did not get back to the gasthaus till three in the morning. The place was all locked up, and the only way in was to climb the trellis to the first floor veranda. The veranda doors were never locked. Then I would walk across the creaky landing floorboards to get to the attic. I did that several times over the months I worked there.

The work was getting heavier by the day. But when I asked the landlady if she was planning to get any more girls to help, I was told to mind my own business.

To test my honesty the landlady used to leave money under the bed. If I put the money into my own pocket I would be classed as a thief, and that would stay in my future reference. No one would employ a thief.

After six months without a single day off I was getting so tired I couldn't keep my eyes open to do my chores. I told the landlady I was leaving. 'Oh no you don't,' she said. I told her that I could not do the work of three people any longer.

She told me I had to give her notice, but I said, 'I am going now.'

'No you are not,' she said, and she phoned the police. By then I was crying.

The police wanted to talk to me on the phone. I told them I was fifteen years old and described all the jobs I was expected to do and explained that I had never been given any time off.

By the end of the telephone conversation the policeman told me to pack my things and said I could leave whenever I wanted to.

So that was another job down the drain. I couldn't stay there any longer; I was drained, totally exhausted. She had worked me to the bone. All for one pound a month.

I had no choice but to go home once more.

I was home for several weeks. I managed to find day jobs, such as potato picking. That was hard work; my back would ache by the time I got home in the evening. For that we got a hundredweight of potatoes for ourselves. Another job was weeding in a field of vegetables – another backbreaking job.

One very hot day, I took my lunch break in the shade under some trees. I was quite alone when an old school friend came walking by. He sat down beside me on the grass verge. I had known him since childhood.

I never expected him to attack me. Within seconds he was on top of me, kneeling on my arms. With his knees he was prising my legs apart. At first I was so shocked I couldn't think straight; he was about to rape me. I really thought that was it, I was going to be raped. The only way out was to trick him. So I let my body go limp and said, 'Why the struggle? Let go and you can have what you want.'

The minute he let go of my arms and legs I jumped up and ran back to the field where all the other workers were. I was out of breath when I got there, and shaking like a leaf. One of the women said, 'What's the matter with you? You're as white as a ghost!'

I couldn't tell what had just happened to me. What could I say - that my old school friend nearly raped me and I had managed to get away in the nick of time? No one would believe me.

My mother was desperate to get me out of the house and into a more permanent job. 'I can't afford to feed you,' she said.

I was now sixteen years old and equally desperate to get out of my mother's way. She was so hostile and angry towards me. The sooner she could get me out of the house the better she'd like it.

When the Hotel Pension Seebover was looking for a kitchen maid, my mother got me the job.

The Hotel Pension Seebover stood in its own grounds by a small lake and was only two miles from our village. I was to work with two other girls: the eldest was Steffani, and then there was Ilsa, who was seventeen.

Our landlords were from Germany. He had been a colonel during the First World War, and his wife, Frau Schneider, was the boss. She ran the hotel business and was a very strict woman. Their son, Schnouzi, was ten years old.

It was a beautiful house with ten guest rooms. Every room had different colour furniture. The kitchen I was to work in was large, to say the least. At one end was a door into a large larder. The door to the larder was always locked because inside was hanging home-cured ham and sausages and home-made salami.

Frau Schneider did all the cooking for her guests. She was a great cook.

The colonel was a portly old man with a white moustache and a bald head. But he was very friendly. Frau Schneider was tall and very skinny. Her hair was black, which she wore in a bun. Her face was wrinkled like brown crepe paper. She had a high-pitched voice and would call us from the garden if we were three minutes late coming back from the garden with the herbs and vegetables. She would stand by the back door of the kitchen and shout, 'Steffani!'

I had to get up at six in the morning to get the fire going in the enormous kitchen stove. Steffani and Ilsa were mainly the chambermaids, but in the evenings Steffani would wait at the dinner tables.

I remember one guest who had a nervous twitch in one eye. It was very embarrassing because we couldn't stop laughing at the man.

Helping in the kitchen wasn't the only job I had to do. I also had to feed the pigs, which were about two hundred feet away from the house. I am ashamed to say this, but I often forgot all about them. When I did remember to feed them, they would scream their heads off to get to the food. The colonel told my mother that the pigs looked more like racing pigs than fat ones.

We would work every evening till ten or eleven o'clock before the work was finished and we were able to go to bed. But we were a happy bunch of girls. We worked hard but we had great fun doing it.

Every Monday was bread baking day. One day, I had been out at a dance the night before and I forgot to salt the bread mix. There were ten loaves of unsalted bread. 'Well,' I thought, 'that's it; I'm really in for it.' The bread tasted horrid. I wondered what the guests would say. But to my astonishment the guests forgave me because I was so tired. Perhaps they realised we never had a day off.

The colonel had a racehorse in the stables. No one exercised the animal and it was so lazy, so I was allowed to take the horse out and ride him.

It was winter 1947. The colonel employed a shifty-looking man from Poland to work in the stables. I figured he must have been running from the authorities. One day I was in the kitchen when he came in. He started fooling around and splashing me with cold water while I was washing the silverware in the sink. He kept on splashing me with cold water. I had a sharp knife in my hand and I threw it at him. I missed by an inch. I was so cross: I had no other clothing; only what I stood in. He walked over to me and hit me straight across my face.

By ten o'clock I had finished the washing up, but I was still in my wet clothes. I then had to walk the two miles to my mother's home to get some dry clothes. By the time I got to bed it was gone midnight.

The next morning there was no sign of the stable man; he had disappeared, like a thief in the night. He was definitely running from the authorities. So now we had no one to milk the cows and feed the horse. Guess what. Yes, you got it right – I got the job of milking the cows and looking after the animals, on top of all the work in the kitchen.

After months of working from six in the morning till ten at night I was so very tired. I was so tired that once I slept for twenty-four hours and no one could wake me.

The only time I ever managed to get some time off was when I told Mrs Schneider that I had to go to church as I was a Roman Catholic. But instead of going to church I went to my mother's house to sleep for two hours. I was really worried that someone might betray me. Once you were found out for telling a lie you would never be believed again, but I really needed the rest: I was exhausted.

Steffani and Ilsa always had boyfriends. I was too immature for a boy to even look at me. At night Steffani and Ilsa's boyfriends would climb a ladder up to our room. They would bring schnapps and music; we had a hell of a time. Frau Schneider would shout from her window, 'Stop making so much noise, the guests are sleeping!'

One night after we finished work we went swimming in the lake without any clothes on. But the boys were spying on us and stole our clothes. It was a good job the night was dark and our house was only just across the road.

I was earning seventy Austrian shillings a month, which is the equivalent of one English pound. It took me six months to save up for a pair of boots, and they weren't even new boots. The rest of the money I earned I gave to my mother. I worked one whole year just for a pair of boots and one dress.

After working day in and day out for a year I needed a break, and the only way I could get that was to hand in my notice and leave. Frau Schneider was very sorry to lose me and she gave me a very good written reference.

So once again I was at home with my mother and the family for a while. But one thing was different: my father was in bed all weekend. He never stayed in bed all weekend. He looked dreadful – gaunt, with black rings under his eyes.

I said, 'Mummy, why is father in bed?'

'Well,' she said, 'I gave him something in his tea.' But Father was so grateful, thinking she was looking after him so well.

I never thought any more about it until it happened

again and again. Father was losing weight, and although he was only forty-eight, he was looking more like sixty-eight.

Chapter Sixteen

It was spring 1948. I was helping my mother on our little farm, herding our goats up in the mountain, gathering wood for the winter. I went to help neighbouring farmers for some extra money, but after a fortnight Mother kept asking, 'When are you going to find another job?' She could only stomach me for a couple of weeks until she got moody, hinting that I was no longer wanted around her.

Fritzi, my youngest brother, was now nine years old, and Englbert was just fourteen. They both still went to school. Fritzi was never beaten with a stick – not like Englbert and me.

The postman brought our daily paper at about eleven in the morning and I would wait for him, hoping that today there would be a job advertised so I could get out of my mother's way. But there was nothing.

Easter was approaching and there were lots of carnivals and dances in different villages. Even my mother and father would come along and join in the masquerade. I often got so drunk that I would stagger home across the fields to our farmhouse at four in the morning. Bear in mind that I was still only just sixteen years old.

It was another several weeks before I saw an advert for a post. It said, 'The lady of the house requires help in the house and tailor shop.' I applied immediately, armed with my very nice reference from Frau Schneider.

The job was in Innsbruck near the Swiss border, quite a distance from my home. I had never been so far away. I would be earning eighty Austrian shillings a month, which was ten shillings more than in my last job. I was on tenterhooks for a week or so, and then the letter arrived. I had got the job!

Innsbruck is a beautiful town. The mountains are so much higher than where I was living. Beck Lodden House was a three-storey corner house. The shop was at the front and the tailoring area was at the rear. The Becks' flat was on the top floor. The kitchen was divided by a partition: that was my room. There wasn't room to swing a cat in my room, and no lock on the sliding door, so I felt quite exposed.

Mr Beck was a tall man with grey thinning hair and Mrs Beck was a petite, round-bodied lady with black hair. She was a no-nonsense woman to work for.

This time in my employment I was actually given a half-day off on Sunday afternoons, which was nice. I could see the town or take the cable car up the mountain.

Every afternoon after lunch I had to go down to the shop where all the coats and suits were made. Mr Beck taught me how to make buttonholes by hand. For several weeks all I did every afternoon was to make buttonholes. Mr Beck also employed a husband and wife as well as a young woman a little older than me. We became quite friendly.

The work was hard. The bed sheets had to be washed in

the bath by hand. And the endless ironing! Mr Beck was very particular about his white shirts. I don't think the ironing board had even been invented then; all the ironing was done on a flat tabletop.

Mrs Beck taught me how to iron a shirt: to do the collar first, then the sleeves followed by the back, and finally the fronts.

I did the ironing just as she instructed me to, but by the time I had the back done the fronts got more creased, and when I ironed the fronts, the back got creased. It was a nightmare, and there were so many shirts to iron. Mrs Beck would say to me, 'What have you been doing all afternoon? You are so lazy.' I could have cried.

After I had been working for the Becks for a couple of months, Mr Beck started coming into the kitchen for a drink of water and then putting his head around my door to say goodnight. That was just the beginning. Then he started to sit on my bed for a chat. What could I do? I needed the job.

As the months went by, he got more courageous. He would try to tuck me in and 'accidentally' touch my breast. I thought to myself, 'Here we go again.' But at least Mr Beck wasn't aggressive – or not yet.

In spite of the situation, I had to laugh to myself. One evening he was nearly caught by his wife. He tiptoed very quickly out of my room and down the hall to his bedroom.

But it didn't stop him coming back for more.

In winter the snow was half a metre high. On my half-day off I would go and watch the ski tournament and the snowy mountains all around the city.

I never told the Becks about my family history. When I was asked about my background I always glossed over things and gave the impression that I came from a 'good' family – not one with a drunkard for a father and a violent mother. But I began to notice that my letters from my mother were being opened prior to my receiving them.

So I was caught out. After that the atmosphere became quite strained. That plus the fact that Mr Beck continued his nightly visits to my little bedroom made me think of moving on. But jobs were very hard to come by, and if you were reasonably pretty you had even less of a chance because housewives did not like pretty domestic maids.

So once again I had no option but to go home to my mother for a spell until something else cropped up.

Everywhere the British were advertising, 'Come to beautiful Britain and get a job.'

'Well,' I thought, 'if I can't get a job here at home, why not go to Britain?' But I was not yet eighteen years old. To travel abroad I had to be eighteen.

Karinthia was occupied by the British; they had taken over hotels, schools and other large buildings. But as the year 1950 approached, some were obviously moving back to Britain. One such family was looking for a children's nanny, an Austrian nanny to go with them to Britain. I saw the advert in our local paper. My mother was all for me going away to a foreign country, but there was still the problem of my age.

First of all, though, I had to get the job. I wrote an essay all about myself and sent an application letter along with my references. Two weeks later I received a reply: they wanted to see me in person. I was shocked, stunned; I was jumping up and down like a mad girl.

The arrangements were made for me to spend a day at their hotel at Lake Woitersee. A small army jeep was sent and off I went.

Mr Newton Dunn was an officer in the British army. He and his wife had three children: William aged nine, and Nicky and Angela were three-year-old twins. The children all spoke very good German, and so did Mrs Newton Dunn.

I did not tell them that I was not yet eighteen. I planned to let my mother sort that one out. I was desperate to get a passport. I would also need a work permit, but that I would leave to the Newton Dunns.

To my joy, I was offered the job. Mother went to our local priest for my birth certificate and told him that the date I was born was incorrect; she told him he had made a mistake and written down the wrong date when I was born. So now I had my birth certificate – and I was a year older.

It took months for all the paperwork to get through the different channels. During that time Mother was busy making coats and dresses for me to travel in.

By the time everything was ready it was April 1950. On 2nd April I was collected from our farmhouse and driven to the hotel where the Newton Dunns were staying. When I said goodbye to my family, my little brother Fritzi was crying; he gave me a wet and snotty goodbye kiss. Father was unhappy about me going so far away. The villagers said they were proud of me to have the courage to go to a foreign country.

I had no idea where I was going to end up in England.

The next morning we got on a special train which was

taking many British officers and their families back to England. We travelled all day and through the night until we arrived at the Hook of Holland, where we boarded a large ship. I had never been on a ship before. I was put in a cabin with two elderly ladies.

I was fine on the train. I loved train rides. We were on the train for twenty-four hours, travelling first through Austria, then Germany, and then Holland. But when I boarded the ship, it really hit me that I was leaving home and going so far away. I cried like a baby. The two elderly ladies felt so sorry for me and were consoling me as best they could, but I could not stop crying.

In the morning of 4th April we docked at Southampton. I couldn't get off the ship quick enough, but it took ages to disembark. When we finally got off we were shepherded into an enormous army canteen. My legs felt all wobbly and I still felt seasick.

Colonel Newton Dunn was provided with a car and we all bundled in. I sat in the back with the twins. I had no idea where I was: somewhere in Hampshire.

We stopped overnight at Mrs Newton Dunn's mother's house. It was late in the evening when we arrived. I was immediately put to my duties: get the twins into the bath.

I tell you, it was easier said than done. The children didn't know me so they would not get undressed in front of me, especially little Nicholas, who was a very shy little boy.

I had looked after my two brothers when they were small. I had never come across children as shy as these.

In the morning I was put to work cleaning the bathroom and the bedrooms. We stayed there for one week and I cleaned practically the whole of the house; they made good use of me.

Eventually we arrived home, which was in a small village in Wiltshire called Littleton Panell. The house had three bedrooms, a dining room and sitting room at the front and a large kitchen. Under the stairs was a small room which might have been a larder at one time: that was my room. At least this was more private than the sleeping arrangements I had had for previous jobs in Austria.

I had sole charge of the children. When they were sick, I had to get up in the middle of the night and change their sheets, wash them and put them back to bed. But I still had to get up at six in the morning to start the fire in the Aga.

But I have never been so well off. I earned twice as much as I had in Austria – not in a month, but in a week. I was rich! For the first time in my life I could buy new clothes. I could throw away the home-made coat that my mother had made me out of an army blanket. I bought new undergarments. I was in heaven. On top of all that I was able to send money home to my mother.

My little brother Fritzi never had any toys so I sent him a toy jeep, just like the one that had taken me away from my home.

Not all the people in the village were friendly towards me; they called me, 'that bloody German'. I heard that a lot. At first I could not understand any of the things that were said. I had no knowledge of the English language, but day by day I was learning. I learned one or two words every day and wrote them down in the little book that I carried about me all the time.

The Newton Dunns made me work hard, but I was used to it. I was clean and quick at any job that was given to me. Angela and Nicky were adorable little three-year-olds, especially Nicky – he reminded me of my brother Fritzi, with dark brown hair and eyes like cherries. I loved him.

On my half day off I could borrow Mr Newton Dunn's bicycle. I would ride around all the country lanes to get to know my surroundings. I went for miles around Wiltshire.

I had never experienced so much rain and wind as I did in England. It felt as though there wasn't a day that it did not rain. But that did not stop me from going out on the bicycle. Any free time I had, I was out, away from the domestic chores.

I was not allowed to sit in the front room in the evenings and my room was small, just six foot by ten – large enough for a three-foot bed and a chest of drawers. It had originally been a larder for storing food.

So in the evenings, after all my work was done, I would get on my bike and cycle through the lanes. I was given a house key but after a while I lost it, so I had to climb in through my bedroom window because I was too frightened to tell madam that I had lost the key. For weeks I climbed in through my window, until someone locked it and I couldn't get in. I had to confess; the colonel was not amused.

I made friends with some children from a council estate. They were fascinated by me; they had never come across someone from another country. They were eager to teach me English. For that I had to sing to them. The Austrian yodel songs were their favourite.

The colonel and his wife would entertain a lot. One of the guests would bring with them Helga, a German girl who was their domestic helper. Helga and I became very good friends. We met as often as we possibly could and wrote to each other every week. Helga worked in Amesbury, Wiltshire, which was quite a distance from Littleton Panell, where I was.

I never spoke any English with the children or the colonel and his wife. That was the whole point – so that the children wouldn't forget their German. But my English was progressing. One day I heard the colonel complain that I had not cleaned the brass doorknob. It was an oversight of mine, but I was always so busy with the children and helping madam in the kitchen.

I was always so tired, particularly as I had to get up in the middle of the night to see to the twins. I had overlooked the doorknob. It felt as though the more I worked, the more I had to do.

Chapter Seventeen

One day in June 1951 I received a letter from Helga. She was in London, having got herself a job in St George's Hospital, Hyde Park Corner, as a maid for the nursing staff. She would make tea and clean their rooms. The hours worked were only eight hours a day, for double the money and one and a half days off a week. Helga urged me to give in my notice with the Newton Dunns and come to London: there was a job waiting for me.

The next day I plucked up my courage and told madam I wanted to give my notice. 'I am sorry, dear Ellie,' she said. 'I cannot accept it. I am responsible for you.' Another week went by and I tried again.

But madam knew she was on to a good thing with me: no English girl would work all the hours that I did.

The next letter I received from Helga was more urgent: 'The job here in London will not be vacant much longer – you must come soon,' she wrote.

The Newton Dunns would not accept my notice to leave, so there was only one option. On my half-day off I took a bus ride into Devizes and made some enquiries about trains to London.

Very early the next day I packed my few belongings, took the six o'clock bus to Devizes and then the first train to London. From there I made my way to Hyde Park Corner and the hospital.

But it had been two weeks since Helga had written to me about the job. In the meantime, the matron of the hospital had gone on holiday, so I was stranded. She wouldn't be back from her holiday for two weeks. I had to find myself somewhere to stay.

So there I was in London. I had no job, nowhere to stay and only five pounds in my pocket.

I had no idea how much trouble I was in. Everybody was looking for me. The Newton Dunns told the police of my disappearance; they also wrote to my mother to tell her that I had gone AWOL. Of course, I had not thought of the turmoil I would leave behind.

For my first night in London I sneaked into Helga's room after dark. The next day I managed to get a bed at the Salvation Army, till my money ran out. My suitcase I left in Helga's room.

I had one more week to go until the matron of St George's Hospital returned from her holiday. Helga couldn't let me stay in her room, so I wandered around London's streets. Men were following me in the park, where I sat down on a bench. I was getting worried.

I began to walk towards Victoria railway station and stopped a little old lady. In my broken English I asked if she had any idea where I could find somewhere to stay. I told her of my circumstances. She took my hand and told me to follow her.

We walked towards a large Catholic church, and beside

the church was a convent. The old lady told me she had just lost her son. She had been coming out of the church when I came along and stopped her. She left me in the care of the nuns, but before she left she gave me her address. I was very lucky to have found the right person to ask.

I was amazed how many girls the nuns had in that dormitory. We all had to work in the kitchen, and the afternoon was taken up looking for jobs. They also charged us to stay there.

Every day I was in touch with Helga. Eventually matron returned from her holiday.

At my interview, Matron was rather sharp with me. She told me how worried the Newton Dunns were at my disappearance. My mother had accused the Newton Dunns of not looking after me, and I was not supposed to look for a job on my own: I was under the government's protection. It was a mess.

I got the job, but I left Matron's office with a red face.

The job was easy: all I had to do was clean the bedrooms of the nurses and the resident sisters. It only took me half the day. The rest of the day I was scratching around for something to do. So I took on extra work, cleaning for the sisters who lived outside the hospital in their own private flats.

I was saving money to go home and see my family. I was homesick: it was getting on for two years since I had seen them. And for some reason even my mother missed me.

Helga and I were like Siamese twins – always together whenever we had a day off. We got to know London inside out. We joined Russian social clubs to get to know different nationalities and people from different cultures. We went shopping for clothes and shoes. We went everywhere together. She was so pretty, much nicer looking than I was.

But, as with everything in life, it came to an end. Helga's family had emigrated to America and Helga was waiting for her papers to come through so she could join her family. In the meantime she was working in England. We had only six short months together.

After Helga left for America I was very lonely. I couldn't walk in the park alone for fear of being followed by dubious men. Many times I had to call for the policeman standing on the corner to rescue me.

At Christmas 1951 I finally had enough money for my train fare to Austria. I bought lots of presents for my family.

It was a long train journey home. When I got home it was so cold: four inches of frost were hanging on all the branches, but there was no snow.

My mother and father pressed me hard not to go back to England, but there were no jobs available other than working on a farm again. I had had enough of dirty old farmers chasing me around the stables and putting their hands up my crotch as soon as I bent down to pick up the washing basket. No thank you.

Christmas came and went. It was a tearful goodbye, as I did not know when I would be able to come home again.

Chapter Eighteen

January 1952. I was back at St George's Hospital in Hyde Park Corner. My room was right under the eaves. My window was on the east side of the building overlooking Hyde Park Corner and Marble Arch. I watched the funeral procession of King George VI from my window. At night the junior doctors and nurses would do their courting on the roof right outside my window.

I was very lonely now that Helga had gone to America. There were lots of Irish girls working as kitchen maids at the hospital but they kept themselves to themselves. They were very religious and went to the Catholic church very early in the morning. They invited me along one Sunday morning for six o'clock Mass. On our way back to the hospital several men accosted us, thinking we were prostitutes looking for business. That was the first and only time I ever went with them.

I only stayed another couple of months at St George's Hospital. In March I found another job at St Mary's Hospital, Paddington. I wasn't in the hospital itself but in a large house for the resident nurses and sisters. The house we worked in was just behind Bayswater Road and not far from Marble Arch. Again, my job was to clean the rooms.

To my surprise there were lots of German, Swiss and Austrian girls working there. We each had our own room. I got very friendly with a tall, blonde Austrian girl. Her name was Steffani and she came from Vienna.

I wasn't lonely any more. We had lots of fun working together.

In August that year I went home again. When I arrived, only my father was there. I found out that my mother had taken a summer job up in the high Alps looking after a young herd of cows which the farmers send up to the Alps for the summer until late September.

I took a bus up the mountain as far as it went, then I had a two-and-a-half-hour walk until I found my mother.

The first thing I came across was a large Alsatian dog, growling at me with his hackles up. I didn't know Mother had a dog. Then I heard the ringing bell of the lead cow. So I climbed on, higher and higher.

When I found her, I did not recognise my mother: she was in rags with a hat pressed down on her head. A tall boy was standing behind her: I did not recognise him at first, either. It was my little brother Fritzi. He had grown so much since I had last seen him.

My mother looked as though she had seen a ghost. I said, 'What's the matter, Mother?'

She said, 'How did you get past my dog?'

I had not for one moment thought that the dog would harm me, so I had just carried on climbing.

Mother said, 'What are you doing up here?' I hadn't told her I was coming home. I had actually left my job in London because I was so homesick. On the spur of the moment I had decided to make another go of being at home and trying to find a job.

It was amazing to be so high up. The view was fantastic. I felt as though I was on top of the world.

Mother and Fritzi were looking after about two dozen young heifers and one milking cow. There was a hut which stood on a plateau. It had just one room and was equipped with a bed, a table and chairs and a stove. Fritzi and I slept under the roof on straw mattresses. They were very itchy. I think there were probably some fleas among the straw.

Mother was quite self-sufficient. She made her own butter, cheese and bread. All that was brought up for her was coffee, which she couldn't do without, and sugar and salt.

I stayed with them for two weeks and then I went back home to my father and brother Englbert.

Father looked old and very thin. He still had his moustache. His big, brown eyes were sunken in his face and his skin looked more grey than tan. From the look of him, I supposed mother was still feeding him poison.

My father never hurt me or my brothers. Mind you, he was never home long enough to really get to know us children. He had been away in the war for four years, and when he was at home he worked in Klagenfurt, which was twenty-seven kilometres away so he only came home on weekends. Then he would go straight out to the gasthaus where he would drink and gamble until he ran out of money.

I didn't look for a job straight away. I just enjoyed being at home, walking the mountains that I loved so much and picking blueberries.

In the first week of October my mother and Fritzi came home from the Alps. She was paid quite handsomely for the three months she had been up there.

I was helping the farmers in the village gather the potato crop. It was back-breaking work, but it was a job.

When the snow came my mother made a harness for the Alsatian dog and put him in front of the sleigh. It was great fun. That dog was very strong – he could pull quite a heavy load.

By Christmas there was nearly a metre of snow on the ground. In London I had bought myself a lot of very fine clothes, including an overcoat from Regent Street. It was the most beautiful coat imaginable. But it was not sufficient for the Austrian winter. My shoes were only made for walking on London streets, not for the snow and slush in Austria.

After the Christmas holidays I started looking earnestly for a job. But every time I had an interview, the lady would look me over with my designer clothes and change her mind. They were likely thinking of their husband chasing the domestic help around the house when the wife was not looking. It was a hopeless situation.

I talked it over with my family. Although they did not like the idea of me going away to England again, I felt I had no choice if I wanted to earn some money. And in London there were many more opportunities to do different jobs. I rather liked the idea of nursing, and there would be no chance of that in my country. The only sisters and nurses you were likely to see in Austria at that time were nuns.

I wrote to the matron at St Mary's in Paddington and asked for my job back. After two weeks I had my reply: she was willing to take me back and get me a work visa/permit.

The only other problem was that I had no money for the train journey. But that is where my friend Steffani came to my rescue. Steffani sent me a train ticket. All I had to do was get on the train and go.

Chapter Nineteen

I set off on 14th January 1953. But I only got as far as Innsbruck, which was where Border Control came along to check our passports. And guess what? Mine had run out.

I was in shock. I had no money, nowhere to stay and the weather was bitterly cold. Thick snow lay on the streets of Innsbruck. The railway station was in chaos. There were people everywhere who were stranded like me, with no place to go. There were Russians, Poles – every nationality you could think of, all stranded in Innsbruck.

That night I was led to a wooden barracks which had rows and rows of bunk beds inside. I was given a blanket and allocated a bunk. I had put my suitcase in storage at the station. I did not want a second night in that cold barracks.

There was a metre of snow on the streets of Innsbruck. My shoes were thin, only meant for summer, and so was my coat. I had not expected to get off the train until I got to England.

I had been in Innsbruck before, when I was seventeen and worked in Mr Peck's tailor shop. I knew my way around the town pretty well. I found what I was looking for: the convent and the nuns. I rang the doorbell and a nun let me in. Her face showed no surprise. She showed me to a large dormitory where dozens of young girls were sitting by their beds. I knew the drill: you work for your keep until you find a job or the nuns find one for you.

The first I had to do was to get my passport renewed. And that had to be done in Vienna. In the meantime I had to send the railway ticket back to Steffani in England and write to the matron at St Mary's Hospital to let her know what had happened.

Now I had to start all over again: to find someone to work for who would get me a work permit. But first and foremost I had to get some money.

I looked through all the adverts in the newspapers. I had several interviews for the position of live-in domestic, but because I was so well dressed no one wanted to employ me. No one wanted to employ a domestic help who was better dressed than the lady of the house.

On one cold February morning a nun came into our dormitory and asked if any of us girls had any nursing experience. I immediately shot my hand up. Secretly I was shaking in my boots, or rather my flimsy summer high-heeled shoes. I had no idea what was involved in nursing an old lady back to health.

I was taken to a high-rise apartment at the edge of the town. The job was to nurse back to health an elderly lady who had influenza. The doctor came once a day and all I had to do was administer her medication and cook light meals for her.

The job was a doddle. I was there two weeks helping the lady back on her feet. I was paid quite handsomely, and with the money I earned I bought myself some galoshes that fitted over my high-heeled shoes.

It had been four weeks and I still hadn't heard anything from Vienna about my passport. But what I did see was an advert for a female servant to come to England – Yorkshire, to be precise.

Mr and Mrs Bowman were on a winter holiday in Innsbruck. The hotel where they were staying was on a steep hill and overlooked the town.

At my interview Mr Bowman told me he was a cotton mill owner in Yorkshire. He was a sympathetic old gentleman, a little on the obese side – he had no neck to speak of – and his voice was oily. I liked him very much. Mrs Bowman, now she was a different story. She was a very stern-looking woman with no smile on her face. But they were willing to get me a work permit. When all the necessary papers had gone through the appropriate channels I could join them at their large mansion in Yorkshire.

I had to go through rigorous examinations. First an X-ray of my chest, then tests on urine and faeces for any diseases that might be lurking in my body. It all took a long time.

By the time everything was in order it was the middle of March 1953. The Bowmans sent me a railway ticket, which cost eleven pounds. I was finally on my way back to England.

I arrived at the railway station in Leeds where a chauffeur of the Bowmans met me and took me to the house. And what a house it was. The road leading to it was half a mile from the main road. It was an impressive sight.

A DIET OF POISON

I stood in the foyer in front of Mrs Bowman. Beside her on the floor sat a sausage dog which looked at me with distrustful eyes. 'You got here, then,' Mrs Bowman said. She showed me my room on the first landing. It was small but comfortable.

She put me to work immediately. There was a lot of cleaning to do: the house was very large. First thing in the morning I had to clean all the fireplaces. There was no central heating, just enormous fireplaces. It took me ages to clean the ashes out and then blacken the surround.

Every day Mrs Bowman would tell me off. I wasn't working quickly enough for her. One morning she told me to clean the bathroom. I made sure that I cleaned every corner. But when Mrs Bowman came home from the shops she told me to clean it all over again.

And that dog of hers, he really had it in for me. He would sneak into my bedroom and rip my nylon stockings to shreds. I hated that dog.

Two weeks after I arrived in England I had an income tax refund of eleven pounds. It came as a cheque which had to be put into a bank account. I did not have a bank account, so I gave the cheque to Mrs Bowman to cash it for me.

Two weeks went by and I had forgotten all about the cheque. One morning I was cleaning the hallway, where there was an enormous dresser. As I was dusting the top, I found a piece of paper, and when I looked at it, I saw that it was my cheque that I had given to Mrs Bowman. She had no intention of cashing that cheque for me.

I have worked for some nasty people in my time but Mrs Bowman took the biscuit. I should have gone to Mr Bowman in the first place.

I was not allowed off the estate on my half-day off. I had no idea where in the country I was. Except for the gardener, the chauffeur and a woman who did the laundry once a week, there was no one else in the house who worked for the Bowmans, and I wasn't allowed to talk to any of them. I felt like a prisoner in the house, and I began to get a little frightened.

After three months of isolation and Mrs Bowman's bullying, I had had enough. I told Mrs Bowman that I wanted to give my notice. At first she didn't accept it, then she got in a fury, ranting and raving about all the things she had done for me to bring me into this country. When she had finished she virtually threw me out of the house.

I went to my bedroom and packed my few belongings. As I was coming down the stairs Mrs Bowman had calmed down. 'Please stay,' she said. But I was too angry. I had decided to go, no matter what.

I waited for a bus to take me to Leeds and then to London. At the station in Leeds I bought a paper and scanned the adverts for possible work. There was one for a nursing orderly in Welwyn Garden City. So that was where I would head for.

Chapter Twenty

I arrived in Welwyn Garden City station late in the afternoon. I had no idea where I was going to spend the night. But the obvious thing would be to head for the cottage hospital that I had seen advertised.

A woman was walking towards me. I stopped her and asked if she would direct me to towards the cottage hospital. She looked at me and said, 'You have an Austrian accent.'

I said, 'Yes, I come from Korinthia.'

She said, 'So do I.'

I was very lucky to have met her because there was no one at the hospital so late in the afternoon. I would have to come back when the matron was in her office.

The Austrian woman took me to her house. She was married to an Englishman whom she had met in Austria while he was serving in the army. I stayed with them for two weeks until I managed to get a job as a nursing orderly. This was the next best thing to being a nurse, which is what I had always wanted to be.

The matron was a very pretty woman, and very friendly. The only person I was not so keen on was the woman in the office. She was Russian and I don't remember ever seeing a smile on her face. I was a little scared of her, and for some reason she didn't like me.

There were four of us orderlies: Margo, who was a German girl, and Megan and Nora who were both Welsh.

I loved my new job. I had so much to learn: how to make a bed and how to give a patient a blanket bath. No more scrubbing floors or washing up. We had maids for that.

Megan and Nora were sharp tongued and a little frightening, but I got used to it and eventually learned to give as good as I got. They wanted to know all my business: where I would go, what I would do and who I would go out with. And if I didn't tell them they got very annoyed.

After I had worked at the cottage hospital for a month I received an official-looking letter. It came from the Bowmans, demanding that I reimburse them for the train fare from Austria to Leeds.

I showed my letter to my Austrian friend who had been so good to me when I had first arrived in Welwyn Garden City. Her English husband worked in the office at Welwyn Garden Stores. He made several enquiries and found out that I was under government protection and that Mrs Bowman had done wrong in dismissing me on the spot with nowhere to go. A letter was sent off, and I never heard any more about it.

Tuesdays and Thursdays were operating days. On Tuesdays we dealt with varicose veins, which were so messy: blood everywhere. And on Thursday we dealt with tonsillitis, usually about six or seven small children.

I dreaded Thursdays because I was the one who had to care for the children when they came out of the operating room still unconscious. I had to watch over them, and if one of the children's faces turned blue I had to get a pair of forceps and pull the child's tongue back out. Otherwise they would swallow their tongue and die.

One day I was feeding an old lady her lunch when she suddenly started swallowing and swallowing and swallowing – and then she was gone. She died right in front of me, just like that – gone. I had never seen anybody die before; it really shocked me.

On my days off I often went into London on the train to do some shopping; I loved going to C&A, the big department store. On the way back to Welwyn Garden City one day I met Donald, who would become my very first boyfriend. He sat opposite me on the train. He asked me, 'Where are you going?' I told him I was a nursing orderly at the cottage hospital. He told me he was a freelance photographer and travelled to London every day.

After that day we spent all our free time together. I met his parents on my day off and spent the night at their house.

Donald and I only had about two months together. He contracted tuberculosis and had to go away for a year. I never saw him again. After that I had dates with a number of different men, but I did not like any of them very much. My mother always said I was too fussy about men and that I would be left with the scrapings of the barrel.

All four of us girls had to take turns covering the night duty. We would do five nights on and two nights off.

On the first floor landing stood a metal cupboard where we would put our coats. But at night, every time I walked by, the cupboard jumped and rattled. It would frighten the life out of me, especially if there was a dead body lying in the next room. People seemed to have a habit of dying between three and six in the morning. Just when it was time for me to go off duty, someone would die and the sister and I had to stay behind and wash and dress the body.

We called the night sister Tallulah. I don't know why the girls called her that. I thought she was weird. I dreaded being alone with her at night. She was small and fragile with mouse-like features and a squeaky voice to go with it.

Sister Tallulah was a sugar diabetic and she had to have her insulin at a precise time every day with a cup of tea. But of course I was completely ignorant about her condition.

One night I came on duty with sister Tallulah and was told to watch a very sick patient in room number 4. He was an elderly man and he was throwing himself about in his bed. I had to make sure he did not fall out of the bed. I was petrified.

Later during the night I went for the sister for help, but when I got to her office she was sitting in her chair holding little pieces of paper in her hands and tearing them into smaller pieces. She was saying, 'What's this? What's this?' over and over again.

Oh God, I had a dying man upstairs and a woman who had gone gaga in her office. And every time I passed that metal cupboard it jumped and rattled; it was a frightening experience.

The sister eventually recovered and the patient died early in the morning. I discovered later that happened quite often with sister Tallulah when she didn't get her insulin on time.

Chapter Twenty-One

Some time later, I met Bill. Yes, Bill was the type my mother was always warning me about.

Bill was tall, big built with black hair and reasonably good looking. At first, everything was fine. We went dancing, Bill took me to the cinema, and he introduced me to his aunt, with whom he was living as he had no other relatives alive any more.

I bought myself a bicycle so we could get about more easily.

We had been going out for a few weeks when one Saturday he took me to a dance at his social club. Bill must have been drinking during the day because he behaved more aggressively than he usually did.

We sat at a table near the wall. But Bill kept getting up to go to the bar and then dancing with other girls. Now and then he would come back to me at the table, and then he was off again. I had had enough. I got my coat from the cloakroom and made my way home to the cottage hospital. I thought, 'No one does that to me – takes me to a dance and then ignores me all night.' I was not just cross; I was fuming.

I was just approaching the hospital when Bill caught up with me. 'Good job I can run fast,' he said to me.

I said, 'You needn't have bothered because I don't want to see you any more.' I went inside and left him standing outside the hospital.

But from then on he gave me no peace. He stalked me almost obsessively.

If I went to the cinema with another young man, Bill would lurk in a corner somewhere, watching me. I tried not to take any notice of him and just get on with my life, but he always seemed to be around.

It was when I was on night duty that I would get really worried. After the pubs closed, Bill would have a fair amount of drink in him, and then he would come to the hospital. The hospital was small and there were no security guards. Bill would stalk the building from front to back, calling my name, 'Ellie!' Then a whistle, and again, 'Ellie!' I was petrified. What if the matron heard him, or the Russian secretary who already had it in for me? I would be sure to lose the job that I loved. I would be sent back to Austria in disgrace. My mother would never forgive me for bringing shame on to the family.

One night Bill was shouting my name and whistling so loud that I had to go down to see him. I tried to calm him down, but he would not have any of it. He started grabbing me and forcing kisses on me. He was a big, strong man, and to resist him was futile. He held both my hands in one of his, and he raped me. I could not cry out for fear of losing my job and the shame of it all.

After it was all over he said, 'Don't worry, you won't get pregnant having sex standing up.' After that, he stopped coming at night to harass me.

After that incident I felt very subdued and lonely. I couldn't talk to anybody about what had happened. I didn't want to go out; I just stayed in my room at the top of the house where all our rooms were. The girls started to tease me saying, 'What's the matter with you?'

My body started to change; my breasts were getting so tender and painful. Then I knew. I was pregnant. After I did my eight-hour shift I would run to my room and cry.

I hated Bill for putting me in this situation. I knew I shouldn't have gone outside in the first place. I left my patient to go walkabout, and I left myself wide open for Bill to rape me. I knew the Russian secretary would have a field day. She was now in charge of the running of the hospital. Our matron had mysteriously disappeared so I had no ally there.

I had no idea what was going to happen to me once my pregnancy started to show. The two Welsh girls would just love to see me getting into trouble.

I went to see Bill at his aunty's house. I told him that he had made me pregnant and that I would be sure to lose my job. He stood there with a grin on his face and said, 'If you have twins we will share them.' That's all he had to say for himself.

I was three months pregnant and on night duty. We had some very heavy patients to lift. I started to have some severe cramps in my stomach. By the time I came off duty I was also losing blood.

I still had the address of the doctor I had seen when I worked in London. I did not dare risk going to a doctor in

Welwyn Garden City. By the time I arrived in London I was bleeding quite badly.

The doctor told me I had to go to the hospital immediately, but the ambulance could not pick me up from the street or from his surgery: it had to be from a house. He said there was nothing he could do.

I was devastated. The only thing I could think of was the nuns. They had helped me before; maybe they would help me again. Otherwise I would just bleed to death on the London streets.

I took a bus to the convent in Victoria and knocked on the heavy door. One of the nuns asked me what I wanted, so I told her about my predicament. She let me in and sat me on a chair in the large hallway, then went to summon the Mother Superior. She seemed to take ages to come, by which time I was bleeding so heavily that a puddle was forming under the chair.

By the time the ambulance came and took me to St Stevens Hospital I had lost a lot of blood and was practically unconscious.

The next thing I remember was being in a hospital bed and people standing around me, shaking me and slapping my face. I opened my eyes but I could see only white fog and ghost-like figures standing in front of my bed. I was so weak I could not even lift my hand.

But the doctors and nurses were relentless. They asked me questions for what seemed like hours, until at last they gave up.

A couple of days later Margo, the German girl from the cottage hospital came to see me. She brought me a nightdress and some toiletries. She told me that the cottage hospital knew about my predicament and my situation was very iffy indeed. Maybe I would lose my job after all.

Chapter Twenty-Two

March 1954 was approaching and my work permit was running out. I needed to find a job very quickly because the secretary from the cottage hospital was unwilling to renew my existing work permit for the year ahead. She wanted to get rid of me once and for all. She had considered me to be a pain in the neck ever since I had started working at the cottage hospital, for some reason or other.

I managed to find a nursing job only a few miles from Welwyn Garden City. This hospital was much bigger. It was an isolation hospital for infectious diseases, called Gallows Hill.

The matron at Gallows Hill looked like Queen Victoria, except a shade taller. Her bonnet was tied under her chin, and she had half-moon glasses which she wore halfway down her nose. 'Now Miss Rohm,' she said, 'I run a strict hospital here.' She was a person to be frightened of.

I started work on Ward 6, with children suffering from measles and tonsillitis, and babies with severe diarrhoea.

I loved working with the children, but it was heartbreaking when they wouldn't take their feed. Every drop of milk had to be measured. I also had to learn to write reports on them. Each child was in a separate cubicle; we had to wash our hands before going in and put on a white coat.

I was working with a Sister Carlyle, Staff Nurse Reed and Night Sister McCarthy. There were lots of girls who were nursing orderlies. And this time there was no bitchiness among us. I made great friends with them all.

We had rooms on the first floor of the main house. Matron had her own apartment on the east side of the great house, and Inga the German girl was her personal maid. She often told us that the matron was a lesbian.

I don't think I had fully recovered from the blood loss and the miscarriage that I had suffered. I was getting very thin and my back would hurt when I lifted heavy patients.

Sometimes I worked on Ward 2, with patients who had different kinds of illnesses. Some were old with severe arthritis; others had tuberculosis and had to lie very flat on the bed. Many were very temperamental. All of us girls had to be inoculated against infectious diseases.

We had to be in by ten o'clock every night unless we had a special pass. I remember running up the hill, sweating in my attempt to be back on time, but very often I didn't make it by ten. And I knew what would happen: I would be in Matron's office again in the morning.

Every Saturday there was a dance at the Drill Hall. It was there that I met Reg Green. He had ginger hair and was very shy, which intrigued me. You wouldn't get a shy boy in Austria. Reg wasn't much of a dancer, so while he was with his friend Johnny Brewster, I was with the girls having fun and very often got drunk. But Reg and Johnny always picked me up outside the Drill Hall and made sure I got home safely.

Matron was always picking on me. Nearly every day she would summon me to her office for one thing or another. One morning I was working on Ward 2 when Matron walked in with the sister in charge. She had us all lined up in a row. I had no idea what it was all about.

'Now, who has got it?' she said.

We all looked at each other.

'I want to know who the thief is,' she said, and stopped in front of me, looking into my eyes.

I felt guilty by not being guilty. She made me feel guilty. She wanted me to be the guilty one.

Apparently, one of the tuberculosis patients had lost some money from her locker and said that one of the nursing orderlies had stolen it. Matron knew that I was frightened of her, which the other German girls were not. So Matron was always on my back. But this time I felt she overstepped the mark, and I had had enough. I went slamming into her office and confronted her. Her secretary stood up and left the office.

After that confrontation, Matron changed towards me. She became much friendlier, but not too friendly. She lent me her sewing machine because she knew I enjoyed making my own dresses. And when I had flu, she even gave me her budgerigar to keep me company while I was recovering on Ward 2.

One day, Matron sent for me and Irene, a German girl. She said, 'You two girls are going to Ware Park Hospital for men's tuberculosis patients to do your night shifts. You will be picked up every night and taken up there.'

I was so nervous: so many young men. I was not used to nursing young men. They would play tricks on us. One of them had a banana on a very fine piece of string. He would say, 'Nurse, please could you pick up that banana for me?' As we bent down, he would pull the string and the banana would go flying away.

Another of their tricks would be to put a mirror on the floor while we were making their beds so they could look up our skirts. They played so many jokes on me that I began to get depressed and started to cry. It was a nightmare taking their temperature: they were always fooling around with us nurses.

During the time I was at Ware Park, I fell in love with a patient. His name was Georgie Regan. He was allowed to walk out during the daytime.

It was an innocent relationship. He was lonely, away from his family, and was a married man. There was no future in this for me. Georgie was eventually discharged from the hospital.

After we had been at Ware Park Hospital for six months, Gerda, Irene and I were sent to work in an old people's hospital Leytonstone in London. The place was enormous – a mass of buildings to get lost in.

In Leytonstone we were constantly under surveillance. Our behaviour was reported back to our own matron at Gallows Hill Isolation Hospital to make sure we were working hard and were kind to the elderly patients.

On my ward I was called 'white wings' because of the way our hats were made – they looked like butterfly wings.

I loved looking after those old people: they were like children, in some ways. One old lady was a hundred years old; she lived entirely in the past. When she wanted to go to the toilet she used to shout very loudly, 'I want a piddle.' I thought that was very funny. I learned a lot of London slang from the local girls who worked with us.

One day the ward sister told me to remove a bedpan from a patient; she must have been more than twenty stone in weight. I lifted up her fleshy, flabby thighs – first the left, then the right, but I could not see the bedpan. I went back to Sister. I said, 'Sister, I cannot see a bedpan.' That poor woman was sitting on that bedpan for hours. It took three of us finally to lift her off.

The London orderlies were very cruel to the patients. I remember seeing one old lady tied up in the toilet to make her sit still. Another was slapped and pinched because she was wetting the bed.

For six months, the wards at Gallows Hill had been undergoing renovation. But now this was finally completed and we all returned to our own jobs, only now the hospital had more old people. The TB patients had all gone and the wards had been disinfected, but we still had the children's ward.

Chapter Twenty-Three

In autumn 1954 I was summoned to Matron's office. I was working on Ward 6 feeding a little baby who was very poorly. I thought to myself, 'What have I done wrong now?'

When I got to Matron's office I knocked on the door and waited until I heard her say, 'Come in.'

As I entered the room there were two police officers standing there. All the time I was thinking, 'What the hell have I done now? Maybe she is sending me home in disgrace like she has always threatened if I did not behave.'

But instead, Matron stood up from her seat behind her desk and left the office.

The police officers told me to sit down and started to ask me questions. Had I received any correspondence from my family? I told them that as a matter of fact I had not heard from my mother for some weeks now. I told them I had written but had received no reply as yet. I hadn't thought any more about it: I just thought she was too busy to write to me.

I asked one of the police officers, 'Why are you asking me all these questions?' but they were very tight lipped and wouldn't tell me anything. All they said was would I come to the police station the following day on my day off.

I had no one to talk to and I was very frightened. I wondered if maybe something had happened to my mother. My father was always beating her to a pulp when he came home drunk from the gasthaus.

The next day I went to the police station. I was shown into a small room that was barely big enough for three people. Two plain-clothed officers sat opposite me. One was very sympathetic, which gave the impression that he was on my side. The other officer was taking notes.

I was there for two hours. Had I sent home any parcels lately? Did I have any contact with any poisonous medicines? I told them I did not; I was only a nursing orderly and did not have any contact with any medicines whatsoever. The staff nurses or the sisters would give medicine to the patients.

I said, 'Why are you asking me all these questions?' But I got no answer.

The questions went round and round in circles. I was so tired and frightened, and still they wouldn't tell me what was going one.

I was told to come again the next day. This time it was in the evening and I took my friend Georgie Regan with me. It helped to have a male accompanying me, but still the police wouldn't tell me what was going on in my home village, especially not in front of Georgie.

I felt so isolated; I had no one to talk to. I had a feeling something very bad had been going on at home. I also realised that I had received no letter from home for a very long time and that my letters to my mum hadn't been answered.

Around this time I began to have some very bad dreams. In one of my dreams my father was chasing me. When he caught up with me he put a rope around my neck, and I could see myself hanging from a tree.

The third time I went to see the police I saw the top man himself. He was very kind to me. He told me that all the enquiries that had been made about me showed that I was free of any involvement. He also informed me that my mother was in prison for killing my father. He was unable to give me any more details as it was an ongoing investigation.

I was so shocked I started to tremble, and I couldn't stop the tears from running down my face. All the way back to the hospital I was crying. Matron gave me a look that said, 'I know all about it.' It was a look that said to me, 'You put a foot wrong and I will send you back to your own country in disgrace.

In the days that followed I kept myself to myself and spent most of my time off in my room. I wanted to go home and see for myself what was going on, but I had to save up the money for the fare home, plus some extra to keep myself. The train fare cost £19 and I only earned £4 a week.

By the time I had enough money saved it was March 1955. I asked Matron if she would be willing to keep my position as nursing orderly open for me and, to my amazement, she told me she would. I didn't want to cut myself off completely. I didn't want to make the same mistake as I had in 1951 when I thought I would stay in Austria for good. But there were no jobs such as nursing orderlies in my home town, or any jobs other than farm or domestic work, and I had enough of that when I was fourteen years old, with dirty old men putting their filthy hands up my skirt.

Over the years that I had worked in England I had accumulated a lot of beautiful clothes, so when the time came to pack my belongings for the journey home, the trunk I had bought second-hand in London was very heavy. Plus I had a bicycle which I did not want to leave behind. When I got to Victoria railway station in London, I sent all my luggage by rail.

My train left Victoria for Dover at two o'clock in the afternoon, and then there was a four-hour crossing to Ostend. In Ostend I boarded the train that went right through Germany, Austria and Zagreb. All in all it took two days of travelling before I got to Klagenfurt. Then I had to take another taxi to my aunty's farmhouse. By then it was getting dark and it was raining.

I had to go to my Aunty Angie; I had nowhere else to go. My home was boarded up and my family were all in prison.

At my aunty's I felt like an interloper. She went on and on about how bad my mother Maria was and how my poor father must have suffered. Of course, she never knew how cruel my father was when he came home drunk and smashed the furniture to pieces, or that we children would hide in the wardrobe while he hit my mother until she was unconscious, year after year. The only respite she had had was when my father had joined the German armed forces.

My uncle John, Aunty Angie's husband, worked as a lumberjack and only came home at weekends. He always brought home fresh oranges and sweets for his seven children. He was a rugged sort of a man and very vulgar. I for one kept my distance from him; he would be quite likely to grab a girl's breast or bottom if she got too close to him.

I was very eager to get to my mother's house, so when my uncle John managed to borrow a small pick-up truck we set off over the other side of the mountain to my home. When we got there, I was shocked. The place was in a mess; all the best pieces of furniture had gone, including my mother's sewing machine. Photos were strewn all over the floor, and all the best clothes and bed linen had disappeared. In fact, there wasn't much my uncle and aunty were able to put onto the lorry to take away – just a bed, a bedside cabinet, a table and some chairs. Even the wood that my mother had collected all through the summer had gone.

My heart was breaking; I couldn't stop the tears from running down my face. It felt as though my whole family had gone in one swoop, wiped out; no more base where I could stop off and see them when I wanted to.

I was on my own now.

After we took the few sticks of furniture to my Aunty Angie's farm I made arrangements to visit my mother in prison. Luckily for me she was still being held in Klagenfurt. My brother Englbert had already been taken 300 km from Klagenfurt, so there was no chance of visiting him.

When I got to the prison I was taken to a very small room. My mother and my little brother Fritzi were already standing there by the window. I hugged Fritzi and all I could think of to say was, 'Why, why, why did you do it, and why did you bring the boys into this mess?'

'Well,' she said, 'at least I know where they are.'

Fritzi was only fifteen years old; they gave him fifteen years for helping her kill my father.

I cried all the way home on the bus to my aunty's farm; I just couldn't stop. My mother didn't even look sorry for what she had done.

Englbert was eighteen years old. He was given twenty years imprisonment and so was my mother: twenty years. Twenty years means life in Austria.

I was so lost. Lost without an anchor.

My aunty was kind enough to let me stay with her even though she had never really liked me, but I was her sister's daughter.

Chapter Twenty-Four

Over the weeks that I stayed at my aunty's I was told the gory details. Mother had been poisoning my father for years, and when that didn't work, she strangled him. Then with the help of the two boys she carried him for a kilometre to the forest where she had a shed. Inside this shed is where he was found hanging from a rope.

Not for one minute did she think she would get caught; that's how naive she was. She thought because she had been abused all her married life she would be given a light sentence for killing my father. She never took into consideration that poisoning him for years would alter the outcome at court.

The little room I was given at my aunty's was no bigger than a tool shed. There was one very small window which had no catch to it, and it was very low to the ground.

And an old man named Jack (he was the village drunk) would look through my window every night on his way home. He would shout, 'Ellie, let me in!' The first time it happened I was frightened out of my wits, until my aunty told me that the old man was harmless.

The whole village was laughing, saying he was coming a-courting. He must have been seventy if he was a day. Sometimes he would get halfway through the window. I was terrified that he might actually get into my room. At first I thought he was just a village idiot, but he wasn't: he owned a large farm not far from my aunty's house.

I had to get some money from somewhere so I sold my bicycle to my aunty and a long black winter coat to my cousin Mitzi, who was fifteen years old. I also did some dressmaking for the local farming families. At one place I had to make a bridesmaid's dress for an eight-year-old girl. I wasn't particularly experienced and I was very nervous as I cut into the satin material. I was so relieved when that job was done; I couldn't let on how inexperienced I was.

My aunty's farmhouse was very old and primitive. There was no running water indoors. We had to fetch the water with buckets from a standpipe across the road. And of course, at that time you wouldn't dream of having a toilet indoors; that stood about four metres away from the front door. It was just a wooden hut containing a bench seat with a hole cut out of it. You could see the human waste crawling with maggots, and the stench was phenomenal.

At the east side of the farmhouse was a stable where Aunty kept a cow, a couple of goats and a pig. Very often Aunty went away to Italy, which was just over the border from Austria, for a few days because my cousin Hansi was a sickly child and needed sea air. So I was left to look after the rest of the family. Milking goats and cows was very familiar to me, from when my mother had had a smallholding.

Ernsti was the youngest of my cousins; he was an adorable little boy: I carried him around everywhere.

Chapter Twenty-Five

Every day at around ten in the morning, Adi the baker boy arrived in his van with bread and sweet buns. He took quite a shine to me. We got talking and he said he wanted to take me to Venice over the Easter bank holiday. I thought, 'Why not? it's better than hanging around here.'

Adi waited for me a mile down the road from the farm. All I had with me was my toothbrush and a change of clothes. It was quite late in the day when we set off on his motorbike because he had to deliver his bread round on the Saturday and didn't finish until four o'clock in the afternoon.

I didn't tell my aunty that I was going away. I didn't think she would approve.

We rode for about two hours and then darkness fell upon us, so we stopped at an old inn for something to eat and a room for the night.

I hadn't really considered the consequences and what it might entail if we had to stop overnight. I was just so excited about the trip. I had never really had a proper boyfriend before.

So when we were climbing the stairs to our bedroom I

was getting very nervous. The room had an old-fashioned bed, over which hung a very large picture of Jesus and the Madonna. I could feel them looking at me saying, 'You are committing a deadly sin.' That is what our Catholic priest always told us when we did something wrong, and I would have to go to confession after that.

I waited until Adi was in bed before I came out of the bathroom. I kept my panties and my petticoat on.

But when I got to the bed I couldn't believe my luck: he was fast asleep, having got up at four o'clock in the morning for his bread delivery and then travelled for hours on the motorbike. He was out cold, thank God.

In the morning, after breakfast, we got going back on the long road to Venice.

Adi was a real country boy; he wasn't the easiest man to get on with. He hadn't been anywhere and knew even less about anything. We argued quite a lot. We stopped every two hours or so for a break; both our backsides were getting sore. At one time when we stopped I needed to go to the toilet very badly. The railway station was just ahead and Adi stopped the bike. I dashed to the ticket office and asked where the toilet was.

First the man did not understand me. I managed to get through to him in sign language. He pointed to a door at the far side.

I knew the toilets at my aunty's were primitive, but what I saw here I could not comprehend. All I saw were two stone slabs, and between the slabs was a hole. I quickly ran outside and went back to the ticket man. I said, 'I want a toilet.' But he just kept on pointing to that small door.

I had never seen anything like that before; that's how

primitive the northern side of Italy was. People still lived in cave dwellings that we could see as we travelled along the road.

Early in the evening we arrived on the outskirts of Venice. We were hungry and tired, and we also had to find somewhere to stay overnight. But everywhere was full because of the holiday.

Adi was asking people for one night's accommodation, and eventually we got lucky. A young man took us to his parents' flat who took people in for extra cash. They lived on the fourth floor of a tower block. Adi paid for the room in advance because we wanted to get going very early in the morning. The room was practically empty, but for two camp beds.

Thankfully Adi was too tired to start any lovemaking, but there was still the morning to come.

Adi wasn't the type of man I liked. We had different opinions and outlooks in life. I had travelled quite a lot and had had to fend for myself since the age of fourteen. In short, we did not get on.

In the morning, Adi woke up, got off his camp bed and climbed into mine. The whole metal frame collapsed. It made a hell of a crash. First we listened to check whether anyone had heard the noise, then we got dressed as quickly as we could and got out of there.

When we got down to the street where Adi's motorcycle was parked, we pushed the bike slightly away from the area so we didn't make a noise.

There was one road into Venice, and a railway. The road was very straight, and either side of it were patches of sand and water where nothing grew but seaweed.

The first place we came to was a large car park for coaches and cars. That was as far as you could go on a motorised vehicle. From there, everyone had to walk or go by water taxi. We walked, as we did not have enough money for a water taxi.

We walked through narrow streets and hump-backed bridges. We walked over the Bridge of Sighs where hundreds of convicts had been put to death. We boarded a water bus to St Mark's Square where there were hundreds of pigeons on the ground. We had lunch at the water's edge. That was about all the time we had before we had to head home. Adi had to be back at work first thing Monday morning.

As we approached my aunty's farm it was nearly midnight. By then, Adi was beginning to get quite frustrated. There had been no opportunity for him to have his way with me, so he was going to do his best to have his way with me now that we were home.

I really did not feel like being molested and having sex on the damp ground after six hours of riding pillion on his motorcycle. So I simply said, 'No,' and went to my little room to sleep.

The next day, of course, there were a lot of questions and snide remarks, such as 'Dirty stopover,' but I let it all wash over me.

Chapter Twenty-Six

It had been three months since I had come home to Austria.

It wasn't exactly a picnic to stay with my aunty Angie. She constantly reminded me how bad my mother was and of the shame she had brought on the rest of the family. She never gave it a rest.

I was also getting fed up with the old farmer coming to my window every night after the pubs were closed and shouting, 'Ellie, let me in!' The whole village got to know about it.

Once more I travelled by bus to Klagenfurt to see my mother and Fritzi, but I discovered that both had been moved. Mama had been sent to Vienna and Fritzi had been moved to Graz where my brother Englbert was.

There was nothing more for me to stay for in Austria. Jobs were non-existent and I had no one left to stay for. My home had been ransacked; all that was left were a few photos and some of my mother's dresses. Everything had been destroyed, and I felt that I had been left in the cold. Even now as I am writing this, tears are flowing down my cheeks.

I had to get out of Austria. There was a contract out on

me: my aunty Angie told me that the relatives on my father's side wanted to lock me up and put me in an attic, like they used to lock up children during Hitler's war, children who suffered from cerebral palsy or any kind of deformative condition.

Before I had left England the matron at Gallows Hill had assured me that my job as a nursing orderly was secure and that I could come back whenever I wanted. My passport was in order and my work permit was valid for another nine months, so I set off back to England, which now felt like my second home.

It was my twenty-third birthday. Matron gave me permission to have my birthday party in our sitting room, which was big enough to hold quite a lot of people.

I invited all my friends, including my best friend Frances and a young man I had been quite keen on before I went to Austria for three months. His name was James.

James was very handsome, and I fell in love with him. I had seen him at the Drill Hall on Saturday nights but he was always too shy to ask me to dance. It was Frances in the end who got the two of us together. I thought to myself, 'Why not? I won't take things too seriously because of my background.' How could I get serious with anyone? They would run a mile if they knew about my mother spending the next twenty years in prison.

A year later Frances got married. Around the same time James asked me to marry him. I was thrilled that I would have a home of my own, but I was also very frightened: would he still want to marry me when he found out about my family back home?

I figured that when the time came I would have to face the questions: are your parents still alive? How many siblings do you have? Perhaps we could go to your country to meet them, and so on. I didn't want to think about it at that time. I put it out of my mind, to deal with when the time came.

I did get married to James; we were very much in love. I told him about my family and what had happened to my brothers and my mother. James promised me that he wouldn't tell anyone, especially his parents who were anti-German and not particularly keen on the idea of me marrying their son.

Married life wasn't as I had imagined it would be. I had always been a dreamer.

I wanted my husband to adore me, to love me more than he loved his own family. But it did not turn out that way. In reality, James loved his family more than he loved me. He spent all his free time at his mum and dad's house, and I was left sitting and waiting for him to come home to me.

At weekends he would say, 'I won't be long – I'll just pop up to my dad's and then we'll go for a ride on our motorbike for a picnic.' I waited and waited and waited some more. In the end I got on my bicycle and went for a ride by myself rather than staying at home on my own. James was so attached to his family he couldn't stay away, ever.

These were the times when I felt very lonely and sad. I would remember that I no longer had a home to go to. Even though it had been an unhappy home, it was still a home. Knowing it was there, the mountain, the place I grew up, it does not matter how far you are from home, at the back of your mind you know it is there whenever you want to see it.

One thing I thank God for is that when my mother told me to come home I ignored her plea. If I had gone home she would have forced me to help her. She had set her mind to killing my father.

My mother was so strong willed it was impossible to say no to her. She was a force to be reckoned with. I would have ended up in prison, as sure as God made little green apples.

I would have never survived being incarcerated. I was too timid to stand up for myself. When I was at school I was always punched and beaten; although I was tall for my age I was thin and undernourished.

When I wasn't being beaten by my mother I was bullied at school; the teacher was ever ready with her stick, and even the Catholic priest used to hit me with his Bible. It's a wonder I came out sane.

Chapter Twenty-Seven

After three months of married life I fell pregnant. It was hard to keep house and to be rushing off to work. As soon as I shut the front door behind me I had to rush back and be sick. I often missed the bus to work.

After work I would rush home to make James his dinner, which he seldom ate because my cooking wasn't up to the standard of his mother's. So I had to cook him something else. By the time I got to sit down it was very late, and I was so tired and my back would be killing me.

I had given up my job as a nursing orderly and I was now working in a toothbrush factory until the baby was born.

It has been three years since I had seen my two brothers and my mammy. But money was tight, building a home and getting ready for my little baby.

I was so happy when Ronald was born. He had beautiful, long eyelashes that all the nurses fell in love with. My husband, too, was so proud to have a son.

One day I received a letter from my brother Englbert. He was having a hard time in prison. His health was failing and he needed some warm clothes and some money. He told me that our mother had had a slight heart attack and that our brother Fritzi hadn't written to her for a long time.

I always wrote regularly to my mother, but it was the letters from Fritzi that she wanted most; they were the only things that mattered to her.

But my brother Fritzi was studying hard for his future.

Frau Schavenstein had helped Fritzi to secure an early release from juvenile prison, where he should never have been in the first place. She worked tirelessly and pulled every string possible to free my brother.

She made sure he got a good education and eventually he was able to take up a profession in architectural designing and drawing, which he had a talent for.

But it took Frau Schavenstein five years to accomplish this.

Englbert was a very sad and lonely man. He would occasionally write poetry:

> I came and don't know where from,
> I go and don't know where to.
> I wonder why I am so happy,
> But that was once but no more.
> *Englbert Rohm*

Two years later, we had finally saved enough money to go to Austria for a holiday. I was very anxious to see my two brothers. Englbert was still in prison but Fritzi had a good job and was lodging with a very nice family.

We had to travel by train and ferry. We left Victoria Station in London at two in the afternoon, and two hours later we arrived in Dover where we boarded the ferry to Ostend.

But as soon as I stepped onto the boat I had to go downstairs to lie down because I got so very seasick. Four long hours I had to endure this boat trip, and I was so glad to get off it. When we disembarked, the train was standing there waiting for everyone to get on board.

I was holding fifteen-month-old baby Ronald in my arms, searching for the couchette wagon that we had booked with our train ticket. It was late and Ronald was getting tired and hungry. All I wanted to do was to settle him down and go to sleep.

The porter came and took our passports so we wouldn't be disturbed when we travelled through different countries during the night.

Mid-morning we had a twenty-minute stop in Munich. I got off the train to get some milk for Ronald, but there was a queue. Suddenly the train started to roll out of the station. My heart nearly stopped. My husband James was at the window, his shocked face urging me to run faster. He couldn't speak any German and he wouldn't know where to get off when the train arrived in Graz. My brother Fritzi had never seen James before so they wouldn't know each other at all.

In my panic I tripped and lost one of my shoes between the train and the platform. Thankfully I just managed to grab hold of the rail on the last carriage of the train.

I couldn't believe it. The last time I had seen Fritzi was when he was fifteen in Klagenfurt, just after his arrest. Now he was a young man of nineteen.

I had seen them both together: Mama and Fritzi standing together at a window in a small room at the courthouse. Mama had been very defiant. For her own selfish reasons she made sure the boys went to prison with her. They were both just teenagers.

Fritzi looked so tall and handsome standing there at Graz railway station. We hugged and kissed and I introduced James and Ronald to my brother.

Fritzi drove us in his car to a gasthaus just outside the town of Graz.

Mr and Mrs Klementschitz were an elderly couple who ran the ten-room gasthaus all by themselves, except for a very busty barmaid. Frau Klementschitz did all the work herself, changing the beds and even the cooking. Over a number of years we became very good friends; they loved baby Ronald. Mr Klementschitz used to sit with little Ronald at the kitchen table and play with toy cars with him. At the back of the gasthaus was a large barn where the cat had her kittens. Little Ronald was in his element.

The first thing I wanted to do was visit my brother Englbert. Fritzi and I went through the large prison doors while James and Ronald waited outside in Fritzi's car.

We were taken into a large oblong room. Englbert was brought in by a guard. He had no handcuffs on; all that separated me from Englbert was a long table. We could touch hands but not hug.

Englbert was twenty-three years old, but he looked forty. His face looked grey and his cheeks had sunk into his face. He looked like an old man.

I was so shocked for a moment I couldn't speak. There

were tears behind my eyes, but I held them back; the time for crying would come later when I was alone.

A few days into our holiday with my family and Fritzi, we made the journey to Wiener Neustadt where my mother was incarcerated. Fritzi and I left James and Ronald in Fritzi's Ford Taurus outside the large gates.

I was very nervous: I hadn't seen my mother in six years. A female guard walked us through long, dark corridors to a small room. We had to wait for nearly twenty minutes. Then the door opened and my mother walked through.

She didn't look at me; her gaze was on my brother. She just completely ignored me. I was so hurt. I had come two thousand miles from England to see her and tell her that she had a beautiful grandchild, and she ignored me.

She didn't want to know how I was or anything about my husband: nil, nada. I thought after so many years she would be pleased to see me. But all she saw was my brother Fritzi, her darling boy.

We managed to go to Austria every other year to see Englbert and my mother, and, of course, Fritzi, who drove us everywhere.

James and I were always cuddling and kissing; people called us lovebirds wherever we went. But it was very one-sided. I was the one giving, and felt that I never received anything back. In all the time I was married to James he never said he loved me; it just wasn't in his nature to actually say the words. I am sure he felt it, though; otherwise he wouldn't have married me.

I was fine with that for a long time, until I realised I

wanted more. I wanted someone to love me the way I loved them.

Also my English was getting better and better every day.

Whereas at the beginning my English and James' mentality were on an equal level, by now James' mentality had stayed the same and I was miles ahead.

James would never take my word for anything. He would always go to his father or brothers to confirm what I had said then he'd come home and tell me, 'Yeah, you were right.' So why not believe me the first time? Was it because I was a foreigner and therefore stupid? It was demoralising that he never believed a word I said.

Over the years it got so bad that I lost my sense of self-worth. It was bad enough my mother always telling me, 'You are stupid.' But I didn't expect my loving husband to treat me like an imbecile.

Chapter Twenty-Eight

In 1960 we moved from a two-roomed flat to a three-bedroomed house that the Council had given us. The saying goes, 'A new house, a new baby.'

In the early stages of my pregnancy I was losing a lot of weight. I looked like a ghost. But after six months I began to get bigger and bigger. I got so large that the hospital said they would have to make a surgical belt for me because my spine couldn't take the weight any longer.

When Kerry was born on 18th July 1961, she weighed ten pounds. My little girl was so beautiful. Her hair was black and long and she never lost her hair like babies normally do; it just kept growing. I had always wanted a little girl with long hair.

It is hard work looking after two children when you are healthy, but when you are in so much pain that you can hardly walk, that is altogether very different. My husband wanted his dinner on the table as soon as he walked through the door; the children were playing me up and I could barely stand up any more.

By the time Kerry was two and a half, I had to go into hospital and have a spinal fusion. That meant that a scraping of bone would be taken from my hip and fused into the spinal cord.

I was admitted to St Thomas' Hospital in April 1964. Before I had the operation I was taken to the plaster room where they made a cast of my whole body.

Back on the ward, the nurses were preparing me for theatre. When I saw the nurse coming with tubes and needles, I began to get really terrified. For twenty minutes the nurse tried to get a tube through my nose and into my stomach so as to draw the vomit from my stomach. In the end she had to give up: I just couldn't swallow it.

My operation lasted eight hours. When I came round I had tubes in every orifice: one to feed me, one to draw vomit, one for blood transfusions and one for bodily fluids.

When I was admitted into hospital I had a thirty-six-inch chest. After the operation I only measured thirty inches, I lost so much weight. But that wasn't all: I was not *in* the hospital bed; I was *on top* of it. I was now lying in the plaster cast that had been made before the operation. It was made to sit on top of the bed, in a frame that was fixed to the bed. I was so high up. I was lying in a coffin-like cast, to which there was also a lid. I was turned over twice a day, to prevent bedsores.

The plaster cast was so cold all around me, I couldn't stop myself shivering. The nurses tried to pad it with cotton wool but the draught would come from underneath. In the end I caught an infection and was given penicillin, but my reaction to that was devastating: my throat closed up and I couldn't breathe. All of a sudden there were doctors and nurses all around me, the windows were opened and I was thrashing and fighting for my life.

The operation didn't kill me, but the antibiotics nearly did.

Ten days later my stitches were taken out. I had seventeen stitches on my left hip where the bone was taken, and twenty-five stitches on my stomach. The operation could only be done from the front. It was the first operation of its kind, so the doctor who operated on me informed me.

At the weekends James would come to see me, and sometimes he would bring Kerry with him. She would stand on a chair to reach me and brush my hair. The children were well cared for by my husband's family.

After six weeks I was taken back to the plaster room. First I was strapped into a harness, which was then hooked on to a pulley that hung from the ceiling. The nurses lifted me off the trolley and hung me up. I was hanging like a puppet. One of the nurses ran out of the room, thinking I had died, so she told me later.

This time the plaster cast was fitted over my trunk and halfway down my right leg.

Then my rehabilitation started. I had to learn to walk, like a one-year-old, with the tears and pain that went with it. Sometimes the whole ward cried with me. I was not able to sit; only to walk or lie down. And that is how I was sent home, in mid August.

My children were still being looked after by James' family, as I was not able to cope. I was barely able to manage the stairs, I was still so weak.

After I had been home for two months, I was sent to a convalescent home in Hastings because of complications. James couldn't take any time off work, so I made the long journey on my own. At least I could sit down now. My local hospital had cut the plaster up to my hip but the rest was still on, and it was very heavy.

I took the train to London and then a taxi to Waterloo station. I was very nervous that someone might bump into me and that I might fall over and not be able to get up.

At Hastings station a taxi was waiting for me, but there was no one to help me get in and out of the train and into the taxi. I got off the train okay, but the seat in the taxi was very low, and with the weight of the plaster cast and my leg still so weak, I felt so sorry for myself I began to cry.

The convalescent home stood on a steep hill. It was a very large house with a fair amount of grounds to take walks, and benches to sit on.

I was taken to a dormitory; I had to share with six other women. This would be my home for the next three weeks.

That first night I couldn't sleep. So many people were snoring and shouting out in the night.

I expected at least one nurse to be employed at the convalescent home, but there was none. No medication was given, nor was any even available.

We were ushered out of the room quite early in the mornings and were not allowed back in until bedtime. I would have liked to have a rest in the afternoons, but no such luck. Other than walking around the grounds and sitting on benches, there was nothing to do. I desperately needed some painkillers, but there were none.

During the second week of my stay my husband and a friend of his came to Hastings for the weekend. The weather was warm and sunny and I was feeling quite happy. It was a Saturday and I was taken into the town of Hastings. We had fish and chips for our lunch, and in the evening I was taken to a local pub for a meal. On Sunday morning we went to the beach, and then to Hastings Castle.

I had one more week before I was due to go home. I was becoming much stronger, and the journey home should be so much easier than the journey down. But I still had to make the journey alone.

A taxi was arranged to take me to Hastings railway station. It was much easier getting out of the taxi than it had been on the way down. I boarded the train to take me back to Waterloo station in London. It wasn't an express train: this one stopped at all the stations. I took a window seat facing the engine. There were only half a dozen or so other people around.

Two stops before Waterloo, all the passengers had left the carriage. I was quite alone. I did not hear anybody else enter, but when I happened to turn my head I saw a man sitting just behind me to my left. At first I didn't realise what he was doing, but when I looked again, I got a shock. He was playing with himself!

I looked around the carriage again and there were only the two of us. My body went rigid. I had no way of defending myself. I looked again and he was only two seats behind me, on the other side. The only thing I had in my handbag that might be of any use was a nail file. If he came anywhere near me I could stab him with it!

There was one more stop to go before Waterloo. I prayed that someone else would join the carriage. The train rolled off and no one had come in. All of a sudden, a group of schoolchildren came tumbling in through the door behind me. When I looked around again, the man had disappeared.

I was still shaking when I got off the train. I reported the incident straight away, but the man had disappeared like smoke into thin air.

Now all I had to do was to take a taxi to Liverpool Street station, and I would finally be on my way home.

A week later I had my plaster cast removed at my local hospital. It was a tremendous relief not to have to carry this heavy weight around any more. What I was given instead was a surgical belt to hold me together. With lots of exercises, I could once again lead a normal life.

I was very happy to be with my husband and children once again.

Epilogue

My marriage to James lasted twenty years. After an unpleasant divorce, I lived on my own for ten years. Without any help from anyone I paid off my mortgage on my little house. It was hard going, but I did it.

In January 1987 I got married for the second time, for another twenty years. He was ten years younger than I was. He had his faults, but he was a very loving and generous man. However, it was a stormy marriage, with lots of fighting and verbal abuse on both sides.

He died at the age of sixty-five after going to a party on Christmas Eve. He had been drinking and fell and hit his head. Two days later, he was pronounced dead.

I was seventy-five. I would never marry again.

Now I live for my children and my garden. A recent stroke has taken most of my eyesight, which means I can no longer drive my little car, which I loved very much.

I am now eighty-three years old, and I still live in my little house.

www.ingramcontent.com/pod-product-compliance
Lightning Source LLC
Chambersburg PA
CBHW060157050426
42446CB00013B/2873